||||MOVE IT!

STUDENTS' BOOK

T0385788

SPLIT EDITION

2A

JAYNE WILDMAN AND CAROLYN BARRACLOUGH

SERIES CONSULTANT: CARA NORRIS-RAMIREZ

Reading and Listening	Speaking and Pronunciation	Writing
The Friends' Club	Asking for and giving personal information	A personal profile
The Olympic Games Superstitious Sports Stars ⭕ Lucky charms ⭕ Dictation	Opinions **Pronunciation:** Verb endings: /s/, /z/, /ɪz/	A description of a sport **Writing File:** Punctuation
The Film Museum Extra Special ⭕ Film extras ⭕ Dictation	Suggestions **Pronunciation:** Word stress in adjectives	A movie review **Writing File:** Linking words
The London Dungeon William Shakespeare ⭕ A history quiz ⭕ Dictation	Reasoning **Pronunciation:** Verb endings: /t/, /d/, /ɪd/	A biography **Writing File:** Ordering information
Paul's Problem Page Supergranny Catches Thieves! ⭕ Police interviews ⭕ Dictation	Showing interest **Pronunciation:** *Was* and *were*; strong and weak forms	A short story **Writing File:** Sequencing words

Grammar • To be

1 **Complete the dialogues.**

1 **A** *Are you* (you / be) the new doctor?
  B Yes, I *am. I'm* (I / be) Doctor Jones.
2 **A** .... (Fred / be) a good soccer player?
  B No, he .... (he / be) a bad soccer player.
3 **A** .... (the books / not be) on the desk, Lucy.
    Where .... (they / be)?
  B Oh, ... (they / be) in my bag. Sorry!
4 **A** .... (you / be) hungry?
  B No, we .... (we / be) thirsty!
5 **A** .... (who / be) the girl with the red hair?
  B Jennifer. .... (she / be) a new student.
  A .... (she / be) in your class?
  B Yes, ... (she / be).
6 **A** .... (this / not be) my CD.
  B .... (it / be) Mark's.

• Have

2 **Choose the correct options.**

1 My house *has / have* a small yard.
2 *Does he have / He has* a new cell phone?
3 We *doesn't / don't* have the CDs. *Does / Do* you
  have them?
4 I *have / has* a pet cat.
5 *Does / Do* you have Lila's email?
6 *She doesn't / Does she* have a green bag.
  Her bag is blue.
7 *Do they have / They have* a computer.
8 The car *doesn't have / has* two doors. It *have /
  has* four.

3 **Complete the sentences with the correct form
of *have* or *be*.**

1 Tom .... my best friend. *is*
2 They .... three cats.
3 My room .... two windows.
4 Kate .... a police officer.
5 Those .... new computer games.
6 That girl .... pretty eyes.
7 He .... at the movie theater.

4 **Look at the pictures. Make questions and answers.**

Picture A

1 she / short hair?
  A *Does she have short hair?*
  B *No, she doesn't. She has long hair.*
2 he / an MP3 player?
3 they / green bags?

Picture B

4 the chair / four legs?
5 the cat / green eyes?
6 the dogs / a house?

• There is/are

5 Complete the dialogues with the correct form of *there is/are*.

1 **A** *Is there* a TV in your room?
  B No, ..., but .... a TV in the living room.
2 **A** .... three eggs on the table.
  B .... three eggs, Mom. .... two.
3 **A** .... four pens on the desk?
  B Yes, ...
4 **A** .... two books on the table?
  B No, ... one book.
5 **A** .... a chair in the living room?
  B Yes, ... a small table, too.
6 **A** .... a magazine on the desk?
  B No, ... a magazine, but .... three books.

• Personal and object pronouns

6 Choose the correct options.

1 Class, say hello to Ms. Walton. *She / Her* is your new teacher.
2 Your DVDs are here. Adam has *them / they*.
3 *I / Me* like fruit.
4 Come to the movies with *we / us*.
5 Jade's happy today. Look at *she / her*.
6 Liam is a nice boy. I like *he / him*.
7 This is Nick and this is Carla. *Them / They* are in my class.
8 *We / Us* get up at 6:30 a.m.

• Possessive 's

7 Complete the sentences with the words in parentheses and *'s* or *'*.

1 This isn't *Angela's* (Angela) watch. It's *Peter's* (Peter).
2 Where are the .... (children) new toys?
3 We're at our .... (grandma) house.
4 This is my .... (sister) room, and this is my .... (brother).
5 Is this the .... (men) room?
6 Lily plays on the .... (women) soccer team.
7 It's my .... (friends) birthday party. They're twins!
8 Do you have .... (Oliver) cell phone number?

• Possessive adjectives and pronouns

8 Rewrite the sentences with possessive adjectives. Then rewrite them again with possessive pronouns.

1 My dad has a big desk.
  His desk is big.   The big desk is his.
2 I have a red T-shirt.
  .... .   The red T-shirt is .... .
3 We have a small car.
  .... .   The small car is .... .
4 Amy and Liam have an old computer.
  .... .   The old computer is .... .
5 Maria has a new cell phone.
  .... .   The new cell phone is .... .
6 You have a nice bag.
  .... .   The nice bag is .... .

9 Complete the sentences with the correct possessive adjective.

1 *His* bag is big.
2 .... bag is small.

3 .... caps are black.
4 .... caps are green.

Vocabulary • Places

1 Match the places on the map to these words.

café *1*	library	movie theater
museum	park	school
shopping mall	gym	zoo

2 Match the words in Exercise 1 to the words 1–9.

1 students, teachers *school*
2 animals
3 trees, bike
4 sports, basketball, tennis
5 movies, popcorn
6 books, study, read
7 history, paintings, art
8 stores, fast-food restaurants
9 coffee, juice, snack

3 Choose the correct options.

1 You take the train at the *station* / *museum*.
2 You play tennis at the *zoo* / *gym*.
3 You go to the movie theater to see a *DVD* / *movie*.
4 You buy clothes at a *store* / *town square*.
5 You have dinner at a *library* / *restaurant*.
6 You have class in a *post office* / *school*.

• Possessions

4 Match the pictures to these words.

camera	computer	dress	sweater *1*
notebook	pencil	radio	shoes
shorts	socks	sunglasses	watch

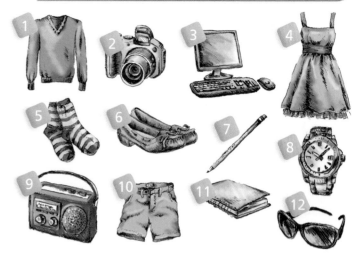

5 Read the sentences. What are these things?

1 You write your homework in it. *notebook*
2 You wear them on your eyes when it's sunny.
3 You take photos with it.
4 You write or draw with it.
5 It tells you the time.
6 You send emails and use the Internet with it.

• Countries and nationalities

6 **What nationality are the people?**

1 the US

2 Spain

3 Turkey

4 Poland

5 South Africa

6 Portugal

1 She's *American*.
2 He's .... .
3 She's .... .
4 He's .... .
5 He's .... .
6 She's .... .

7 **Complete the sentences with the correct country or nationality.**

1 Irina is from Russia. She's *Russian*.
2 James is from Britain. He's .... .
3 Hanna is from .... . She's German.
4 Nadine is from France. She's .... .
5 Matias is from .... . He's Argentinian.
6 Sophia is from .... . She's Greek.
7 Marco is from Italy. He's .... .
8 Karla is from .... . She's Mexican.

8 **What about you? Complete the sentences.**

I am from .... . I am .... .

• People

9 **Read about Zak. Look at the photo below. What does Zak have?**

This is Zak. He is American. He is from Chicago, a big city in the US. Zak and his family are moving to Texas. Today Zak is packing his things.

1 *poster*

Reading

1 Read The Friends' Club.

1.2

The Friends' Club

Jody ⊗

Hi, I'm Jody and I'm fourteen years old. I have a brother, Harry, and a cat. Carlos and Nadia are my friends. We go to school together. I love movies. I have a video camera, and I make movies.

Nadia

My name's Nadia and I'm fourteen. I love dancing, music and fashion. This is a photo of me. I have a sister, Zahra. She works in a store. She's eighteen.

Carlos

I'm Carlos and I love sports. I'm thirteen years old. My dad's Brazilian and my mom's British. I have one brother, Paulo. I'm funny and good-looking. (OK, I'm joking!) My favorite food is chocolate!

2 Read The Friends' Club again. Are the statements true (T) or false (F)?

1 Jody's fourteen years old. *T*
2 She has a pet.
3 Nadia likes dancing.
4 She has a brother.
5 Carlos's mom and dad are Brazilian.
6 Carlos's favorite food is salad.

3 Who is it?

1 *Carlos* has a brother. His name is Paulo.
2 .... has a camera.
3 .... is funny.
4 .... has a sister, Zahra.
5 .... works in a store.
6 .... is thirteen years old.

Writing

4 Make your profile for The Friends' Club.

← → C 🏠   ⊗

👤 **New Member**

I'm .... and I'm .... years old.

I have .... .

I'm .... .

I like .... .

Speaking and Listening

5 Listen. Choose the correct options.

1.3

Jody	Hi, Carlos. What do you have this morning? I have art with Nadia.
Carlos	Lucky you! I have ¹ *science / math*.
Zak	² *I'm sorry. / Excuse me.* What classroom is this?
Jody	It's classroom 15.
Zak	Oh, right! It's my first day and I'm lost. I'm Zak, by the way.
Jody	Hi, Zak. I'm Jody, and this is Carlos.
Carlos	Are you from around here, Zak?
Zak	No, I'm not. I'm ³ *for / from* Chicago.
Carlos	Wow! That's ⁴ *cool. / OK.* I was born here, but my dad's Brazilian.
Jody	Well, guys, I have art now. ⁵ *See you later. / Goodbye.*
Carlos	What class do you have this morning, Zak?
Zak	Er, science. I'm in Room 21a. Where's that?
Carlos	Follow me! We're in the same class.

6 Act out the conversation in groups of three.

7 Complete the conversation. Then listen and check.

1.4

Gabriella	Hi, I'm Gabriella. ¹ c
Adam	My name's Adam.
Gabriella	² .....
Adam	I'm fourteen.
Gabriella	³ .....
Adam	I'm from Poland. What about you?
Gabriella	I'm from Italy.
Adam	⁴ .....
Gabriella	I'm an only child. ⁵ .....
Adam	I have a brother. He's sixteen years old.

a Where are you from?
b How old are you?
c What's your name?
d What about you?
e Do you have any brothers or sisters, or are you an only child?

8 In pairs, practice the conversation in Exercise 7. Replace the words in purple with your own information.

My assessment profile: page 127

1 Play the Game!

Grammar
Present simple; Verb + -ing;
Adverbs of frequency

Vocabulary
Sports; Compound nouns

- Speaking
- Opinions
- Writing
A description of a sport

Word list page 43
Workbook page 116

Vocabulary • Sports

1 Listen and repeat. Then match the photos to twelve of these sports.
1.5

archery	basketball	gymnastics	horseback riding	ice hockey
ice skating	judo	mountain biking	skateboarding	skiing
snowboarding	soccer	swimming *1*	tennis	track

 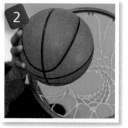  

 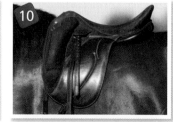

4 Complete the sentences with *play*, *go* or *do*.

1 I *play* soccer with my friends.
2 Paul and Sam .... track at school.
3 They .... swimming in summer.
4 We .... gymnastics in our free time.
5 My brothers .... skateboarding in the street.
6 Claire and Victoria .... judo at the gym.
7 I .... ice hockey in the fall.
8 They .... basketball in the park.
9 We .... skiing in the winter.
10 I .... horseback riding in the country.

5 In pairs, ask and answer. Do you like sports?

> Yes, I do archery and I go mountain biking. What about you?

> I play tennis and I go snowboarding in the winter.

2 Which sports in Exercise 1 are not in the photos?

3 Put the sports in Exercise 1 in the correct column.

play	go + -ing	do
basketball	horseback riding	archery

**Brain Trainer
Activity 3**
Go to page 58

Reading

1 Look at the photos a–c. Which one shows …

1 the Olympic flag?
2 the Olympic torch?
3 the opening ceremony of the Olympic Games?

2 Read the magazine article. Answer the questions.

1.6
1 How often are the Olympic Games?
   Every four years.
2 Are the Summer Olympic Games and the Winter Olympic Games in the same year?
3 Is archery an Olympic sport?
4 When are the Paralympics?
5 Why are there five rings on the Olympic flag?
6 Why are the colors of the Olympic flag blue, black, red, yellow and green?

3 What about you? In pairs, ask and answer.

1 What is your favorite Olympic sport?
2 How many Olympic sports can you name?
3 How many Olympic athletes can you name?

> What is your favorite Olympic sport?

> My favorite Olympic sport is soccer. What about you?

The Olympic Games

Summer Olympic Games

2000	2004	2008	2012	2016
Sydney, Australia	Athens, Greece	Beijing, China	London, UK	Rio de Janeiro, Brazil

Winter Olympic Games

1998	2002	2006	2010	2014
Nagano, Japan	Salt Lake City, US	Turin, Italy	Vancouver, Canada	Sochi, Russia

The Olympic Games are an international sports event. There are Summer Olympic Games and Winter Olympic Games. They take place every four years in a different country. The Summer and Winter Olympic Games do not happen in the same year.

At the Summer Olympic Games, athletes from five continents compete in many sports, including archery, track, gymnastics, swimming, soccer and basketball. At the Winter Olympic Games, the sports include ice hockey, skiing and snowboarding. The Paralympics take place in the same year as the Summer Olympic Games. The Paralympics are for athletes with physical disabilities.

The rings on the Olympic flag are the symbol of the Games. There are five rings because there are Olympic athletes from five continents: Europe, Asia, Oceania, Africa and the Americas. The rings are blue, black, red, yellow and green because every country has one of these colors on its national flag.

The Olympic Games begin with an opening ceremony. In the ceremony, a man or woman lights the Olympic torch. The fire for the torch always starts in Ancient Olympia in Greece. The sun starts the fire in a mirror, and then a woman lights the torch. After that, different people carry the torch to the opening ceremony. The torch visits many countries and towns before the opening ceremony.

Grammar • Present simple

Affirmative		
I/You/We/They He/She/It	watch watches	TV.

Negative		
I/You/We/They He/She/It	don't (do not) watch doesn't (does not) watch	TV.

Questions and short answers	
Do I/you/we/they watch TV?	Yes, I/you/we/they do. No, I/you/we/they don't.
Does he/she/it watch TV?	Yes, he/she/it does. No, he/she/it doesn't.

Wh questions	
I/You/He/She/It/We/They	What shows do you watch?

Time expressions		
every day	on Tuesday	on the weekend
after school	in the morning	at night

Grammar reference page 108

Watch Out!

play → plays   go → goes   study → studies

1 Study the grammar table. Match the rules (1–2) to the examples (a–b).

1 We use the Present simple to talk about routines and habits.
2 We use the Present simple to talk about things that are true in general.
a *My grandfather likes music.*
b *We play tennis after school.*

2 Complete the sentences with the Present simple form of these verbs.

charge   ~~do~~   get up   go   play   study   work

1 We *do* judo on Friday evenings.
2 They .... skateboarding after school.
3 She .... in a hospital near Los Angeles.
4 The students .... French and German at school.
5 You .... baseball on weekends.
6 I .... my cell phone every day.
7 Mom .... at seven every morning.

3 Complete the sentences with the negative form of the Present simple.

1 We like soccer. They *don't like soccer.*
2 I get up at seven. She .... .
3 You study in the bedroom. I .... .
4 She walks to school in the morning. We .... .
5 They go to the movies every Saturday. He .... .
6 He plays tennis every Tuesday. You .... .

4 Make questions with the Present simple. In pairs, ask and answer.

1 you / watch / sports / on TV?
  Do you watch sports on TV? Yes, I do.
2 your dad / wear / jeans / to work?
3 you / study / Japanese?
4 your mom / speak / English?
5 your friends / watch / videos / on YouTube?
6 your teacher / use / computers?

5 Complete the text with the verbs in the Present simple.

Leela's parents [1] *play* tennis every weekend, but Leela [2] .... (not like) tennis and she [3] .... (not play) it. So what sport [4] .... (she / do) to stay fit? She [5] .... (play) soccer. Leela's older sister, Lisa, also [6] .... (love) the game, and the two sisters [7] .... (get) up early every morning and [8] .... (practice) for half an hour before school. [9] .... (their parents / join) them? No, but they [10] .... (not stop) them!

Pronunciation
Verb endings: /s/, /z/, /ɪz/

6 Listen and repeat the sentences.
1.7 Pay attention to the verb endings.

1 /s/:   Grace likes ice skating.
2 /z/:   Baz loves track.
3 /ɪz/:   Liz watches sports on TV.

• Verb + -ing

Affirmative
She enjoys/hates/likes/loves playing soccer.

Negative
She doesn't (does not) like/doesn't (does not) mind playing soccer.

Questions
Does she like playing soccer?

Grammar reference page 108

7 Study the grammar table. Choose the correct option to complete the rule.

After *enjoy, hate, like, love* and *don't mind*, we use the *infinitive form* / *-ing form* of the verb.

8 Put these verbs in the correct order.

don't like   don't mind   enjoy   like

love ⟶ hate

9 Make sentences with the verbs in the *-ing* form.

1 she / enjoy / read / books
   She enjoys reading books.
2 I / not mind / clean up / my bedroom
3 you / like / go / to the movies?
4 we / hate / play / soccer / in the winter!
5 he / enjoy / read / books?

10 Complete the conversation with the correct form of
1.8 the verbs. Then listen and check.

Amy Why do you like ¹ *going* (go) snowboarding, Ben?
Ben Well, I love ² .... (move) on the snow.
Amy Do you enjoy ³ .... (listen) to music when you go snowboarding?
Ben Yes, I do. I like Linkin Park.
Amy Do you mind ⁴ .... (practice) every day?
Ben No, I don't, and I love ⁵ .... (win) snowboarding competitions!
Amy What don't you like?
Ben I don't like ⁶ .... (lose) competitions!

11 What about you? In pairs, ask and answer.

1 What sports do/don't you like doing?
2 Do you mind losing a competition or a game?

Vocabulary • Compound nouns

1 Match the pictures to these compound nouns.
1.9 **Then listen, check and repeat.**

basketball court	football field	hockey stick
ice skates	ice skating rink	judo belt
soccer cleats	soccer field *1*	swimming pool
swimsuit	tennis court	tennis racket

Word list page 43
Workbook page 116

2 Choose the correct options.

1 You play basketball on a basketball *field* / *court*.
2 You play soccer on a soccer *field* / *court*.
3 You go ice skating at an ice skating *rink* / *track*.
4 You play tennis on a tennis *court* / *rink*.

3 Complete the text with the words in Exercise 1.

Holly loves sports. She does judo on Mondays. She is good at it, and she has a brown judo ¹ *belt*. On Wednesdays she goes swimming. She takes her ² .... to the swimming ³ .... . On Thursday she plays ice hockey. She uses her hockey ⁴ .... . On Friday she plays tennis. She needs her tennis ⁵ .... . On Saturday she watches soccer on TV!

Brain Trainer
Activity 4
Go to page 58

Chatroom Opinions

Speaking and Listening

1 Look at the photo. Answer the questions.

1 Where are Zak, Carlos and Nadia?
2 Why do you think they are there?
3 What does Carlos have in his hands?
4 What do you think Zak is doing?

2 Listen and read the conversation. Check your answers.
1.10

3 Listen and read again. Answer the questions.
1.10
1 Does Nadia usually come to the soccer field on Saturdays?
No, she doesn't usually come to the soccer field on Saturdays.
2 Why is Nadia at the soccer field today?
3 What does Zak like about Texas?
4 What doesn't Zak like about Texas?
5 What is the name of Zak's favorite basketball team?
6 Does Nadia's dad like basketball?

4 Act out the conversation in groups of three.

Zak	I quit! I hate playing this game!
Carlos	Cheer up, Zak! You can learn. Now come and say hi to Nadia. She doesn't usually come to the soccer field on Saturdays, but she wants to meet you.
Zak	Hi, Nadia. I'm Zak. I'm from Chicago.
Nadia	Yes, I know. So, what do you think of Texas?
Zak	Well, I think the people are great, but I don't like soccer.
Nadia	What sports do you like?
Zak	Basketball! The Chicago Bulls is my favorite team.
Nadia	Hey, I know the Chicago Bulls. My dad's a fan.
Carlos	I love them, too.
Zak	Then come to my house tonight. We can watch a game together.
Nadia	Good idea!

Say it in your language …

I quit!

Cheer up!

5 **Look back at the conversation. Who says what?**

1 I hate playing this game. *Zak*
2 What do you think of Texas?
3 I think the people are great.
4 The Chicago Bulls is my favorite team.
5 I love them, too.

6 **Read the phrases for asking for and giving opinions.**

Asking for opinions	Giving opinions
What do you think of …?	I think … is/are boring/ OK/great/amazing.
Do you like …?	I like/don't like … … is my favorite team/is my favorite player.

7 **Listen to the conversations. Act out the**
1.11 **conversations in pairs.**

Zak What do you think of [1] tennis?
Carlos I [2] love it. [3] John Isner is my favorite [4] player.

Carlos What do you think of [1] basketball?
Zak I [2] like it. [3] Taj Gibson is my favorite [4] player.

8 **Work in pairs. Replace the words in purple in Exercise 7. Use these words and/or your own ideas. Act out the conversations.**

> What do you think of football?

> I like it. Peyton Manning is my favorite player.

1 track / basketball / soccer / ice hockey / swimming / tennis

2 like / love / don't like / hate

3 Rafael Nadal / Peyton Manning / Taj Gibson / Usain Bolt / Dallas Cowboys

4 athlete / player / team

Grammar • Adverbs of frequency

0%	50%	100%
never / hardly ever	sometimes / often	usually / always
I never see you here on the weekend.	I sometimes get up early.	I'm usually at home on Saturdays.

Grammar reference page 108

1 **Study the grammar table. Choose the correct options to complete the rules.**

1 Adverbs of frequency go *before* / *after* the verb *to be*.
2 Adverbs of frequency go *before* / *after* other verbs.

2 **Put the adverbs of frequency in the correct place in the sentences.**

1 Pete gets up early. (usually)
  Pete usually gets up early.
2 He plays computer games before breakfast. (sometimes)
3 He meets Paul for a game of tennis on the weekend. (often)
4 They play tennis in the park. (always)
5 Pete loses a game. (hardly ever)
6 Their friend Maria is there to watch them. (never)
7 Peter and Paul are happy about that. (usually)

3 **Make questions with adverbs of frequency.**

1 when / you / usually / play / tennis?
  When do you usually play tennis?
2 you / sometimes / go / to football games?
3 you / always / watch / TV / after school?
4 you / often / play / computer games / at home?
5 where / you / usually / meet / your friends?

4 **What about you? Answer the questions in Exercise 3.**

> When do you usually play tennis?

> I usually play tennis on Fridays after school.

Reading 🎧

1 **Look at the photos of sports stars. Answer the questions.**

1 What sports do they play?
2 What are their names?

Superstitious Sports Stars

Many sports stars are superstitious. They believe in good and bad luck. Some have a lucky charm (something they have with them for good luck) or wear lucky clothes. Others believe special numbers are lucky, and some do special rituals (things they do for good luck) on the day of an important game.

Serena Williams, the tennis player, ties her shoelaces in the same way before every match. She often wears the same socks at all the matches in a tournament. She also has lucky shoes and likes having an extra dress with her. Another tennis star, Rafael Nadal, places two water bottles in exactly the same position next to the tennis court before every match. When he wins a tournament, he always bites the trophy!

The basketball player Jason Terry, in addition to wearing multiple pairs of socks while he plays, always sleeps wearing the shorts of the opposing team the night before a game.

Kolo Touré is always the last player onto the soccer field before a game. It's his ritual. Many soccer players believe numbers like 11, 22 or 33 on a player's shirt are good luck, and they think it is bad luck to change their number when they go to another team.

Formula One racing driver, Sebastian Vettel doesn't have a special ritual, but he has lucky charms. He has a necklace and a little metal pig!

Key Words	
superstitious	(good/bad) luck
lucky charm	ritual
shoelaces	trophy

2 **Read and check your answers to Exercise 1.**

3 **Read the article again. Who has …**
1.12
1 a lucky charm? *Sebastian Vettel*
2 a lucky number?
3 lucky clothes?
4 a special ritual?

4 **Read the magazine article again. Answer**
1.12 **the questions.**

1 What does Serena Williams do before a match?
She ties her shoelaces in the same way before every match.
2 What does Nadal do when he wins a competition?
3 What does Jason Terry wear the night before a game?
4 What is Kolo Touré's ritual?
5 What numbers are lucky for many soccer players?
6 What are Sebastian Vettel's lucky charms?

Listening 🎧

1 **Listen to the radio show about lucky charms.**
1.13 **Put the charms in the order you hear about them.**

2 **Listen to the radio show again. Choose the**
1.13 **correct options.**

1 Speaker 1 uses his lucky charm at *school / home.*
2 His lucky charm *really helps / doesn't really help.*
3 Speaker 2 *never / sometimes* loses her charm.
4 She puts it in her *bag / hand* for good luck.
5 Speaker 3 says her lucky charm is *not very / very* lucky.
6 She has her lucky charm with her *every day / on her birthday.*

Writing • A description of a sport

1 **Read the Writing File.**

> **Writing File** Punctuation
> **We use:**
> - a period **.** at the end of sentences.
> - a comma **,** in the middle of a sentence before a new idea, or in lists.
> - an exclamation point **!** to show surprise.
> - a question mark **?** at the end of questions.
> - an apostrophe **'** for possessives (*Rose's MP3 player*) and contractions (*isn't*).

2 **Read about Isabella's favorite sport. Find:**

1 a period.
2 a comma.
3 an exclamation point.
4 a question mark.
5 an apostrophe.

My Favorite Sport by Isabella

I live in Switzerland, and my favorite sport is snowboarding. It's a winter sport, and it's difficult to do in the summer, but from November to April I go snowboarding every weekend with my friends. There are many ski resorts in my country, but I usually go to Verbier. The snow is great there, and I hardly ever go to other places.

The main equipment for snowboarding is a snowboard and special snowboard boots. I always wear a helmet, goggles for my eyes and gloves. My favorite snowboarder is Shaun Roger White. He snowboards in the Winter Olympic Games. He has two gold medals! I think he is an amazing athlete.

Snowboarding is a great sport. It's fast and exciting. I love snowboarding! What about you?

3 **Put the correct punctuation in the sentences.**

1 I have a tracksuit some sneakers and a football
I have a tracksuit, some sneakers and a football.
2 When do they watch soccer on TV
3 Do you have a lucky number
4 Thats Jodys brothers skateboard
5 Mikes brother is a great baseball player

4 **Read about Isabella's favorite sport again. Answer the questions.**

1 What is Isabella's favorite sport? *Snowboarding*
2 Where does she do this sport?
3 What equipment do you need for this sport?
4 Why does Isabella like the sport?

5 **Think about a sport you like. Answer the questions. Take notes.**

1 Which sport do you like?
2 When and where do you play/watch it?
3 What is your favorite team?
4 Who is your favorite player?
5 Why do you like the sport?

6 **Write a description of your favorite sport. Use "My favorite sport" and your notes from Exercise 5.**

> **My favorite sport**
>
> 1 Name of sport and where you watch/play it
> *My favorite sport is* (name) .... .
> *I play it / watch it* (where) .... *with* (who) .... (when) .... .
> 2 Your favorite team and/or player
> *I really like* .... .
> *My favorite* .... .
> 3 Why you like the sport
> .... *is great.*
> *It's always* .... .

> **Remember!**
> - Use periods, commas, exclamation points, question marks and apostrophes.
> - Use the vocabulary in this unit.
> - Check your grammar and spelling.

Grammar • Review

1 Complete the sentences with the verbs in the Present simple.

1 *Do you go* (you / go) swimming on the weekend?
2 We .... (play) tennis every Friday.
3 .... (Jane / walk) to school every day?
4 Gary .... (go) snowboarding in the winter.
5 I .... (not watch) sports on TV.
6 What clothes .... (they / wear) for judo?

2 Complete the sentences with the correct form of these verbs.

lose	~~play~~	play	watch	wear	win

Luke loves ¹ *playing* baseball, and he loves ² .... !
His team usually wins, but when they lose,
Luke isn't happy! He hates ³ .... ! Bella, his sister,
doesn't like ⁴ .... ball games, but she doesn't mind
⁵ .... them on TV. She also likes ⁶ .... her New England
soccer shirt. She thinks it's a great shirt!

3 Put the words in the correct order.

1 play / basketball / usually / after school / They
They usually play basketball after school.
2 a soccer shirt / I / often / wear
3 usually / are / Fast sports / exciting
4 eat / We / never / before swimming
5 He / his friends / often / on Sunday / calls
6 in the park / She / sometimes / studies

Vocabulary • Review

4 Look at the pictures. Complete the sentences.

1 Josh and Alex do *archery* on the weekend.
2 Sasha does .... at school.
3 Max plays .... every winter.
4 Ben and Katie go .... in the summer.
5 Hannah does .... on Fridays.
6 Fred goes .... on Saturdays.

5 Complete the sentences with these words.

court (x2)	~~field~~	pool	rink

1 You play soccer on a soccer *field*.
2 They play basketball on a basketball .... .
3 You go ice skating at the ice skating .... .
4 You play tennis on a tennis .... .
5 He goes swimming at the swimming .... .

Speaking • Review

6 Complete the conversation with these words.
1.14 Then listen and check.

don't	favorite	like	think	~~What~~

A *What* do you think of the Olympic Games?
B I .... like them. I think they're boring.
A But do you .... Usain Bolt?
B Yes, I do. I .... he's amazing.
A He's my .... athlete, too.

Dictation

7 Listen and write in your notebook.
1.15

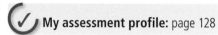
✓ **My assessment profile:** page 128

Math File

Soccer Ball Fact File

You can see soccer balls on the street, in stores, at school and in your house. But what do you know about soccer balls? Here are some facts.

What shape is the average soccer ball?
It's a sphere, and it has a circumference of 68 to 70 centimeters. It usually weighs between 410 and 450 grams.

An average soccer ball has 32 pieces of material:
12 pentagons and 20 hexagons.

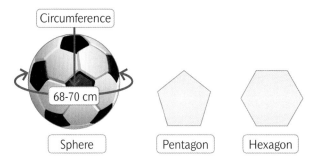

Circumference

68-70 cm

Sphere   Pentagon   Hexagon

There are five different sizes of soccer balls.

Size 1   Size 2   Size 3   Size 4   Size 5

Size 1: This has a circumference of 43 centimeters.

Size 2: This has a circumference of 56 centimeters; it weighs a maximum of 280 grams. This is a good soccer ball for young children. This ball is good for soccer skills practice, too.

Size 3: This ball weighs a maximum of 340 grams. It has a maximum circumference of 61 centimeters.

Size 4: This ball weighs a maximum of 370 grams. It has a maximum circumference of 66 centimeters. Boys and girls from 8 to 12 usually play with this soccer ball.

Size 5: This is the ball for adult soccer games and tournaments like the World Cup. It has a circumference of 71 centimeters.

Reading

1 Look quickly at the text. What do you think it is about?

1 The soccer World Cup.
2 The history of soccer balls.
3 The size and shape of soccer balls.

2 Read the text. Answer the questions.

1.16
1 What shape is a soccer ball? *A soccer ball is a sphere.*
2 How many pieces of material are there in an average soccer ball?
3 What shape are the pieces of material in an average soccer ball?
4 Which soccer ball is good for young children?
5 What does a size 4 soccer ball weigh?
6 Which soccer ball do players use in the World Cup?

My Math File

3 Take notes about some sports equipment you use or your favorite sports star uses. Think about:

- size
- shape
- color
- weight

4 Write a fact file about the sports equipment. Add pictures or photos. Use your notes from Exercise 3 to help you.

The Big Picture

Grammar
Present continuous;
Present simple

Vocabulary
Types of movies;
Adjectives

■ Speaking
■ Suggestions

Writing
A movie review

Word list page 43
Workbook page 117

Vocabulary • Types of movies

1 Listen and repeat. Then match the photos to eight of these types of movies.
1.17

action	animation	comedy	documentary	fantasy	historical
horror	martial arts	musical	science fiction	war	western *1*

2 Which words in Exercise 1 are not in the photos? Think of a movie for each movie type.

Comedy – Night at the Museum

3 Read the sentences. What type of movies are they?

1 Joe likes cartoons. *animations*
2 I like adventures.
3 The songs in this movie are great.
4 I like movies with information about animals, people and places.
5 I love stories about the past.
6 The aliens are cool!
7 There are werewolves and zombies.
8 Cowboy movies are my favorite.
9 It's really funny. There are a lot of jokes.
10 I love watching kung fu and karate movies.

4 In pairs, ask and answer. What type of movies do you like?

What type of movies
do you like?

I like action movies
and animations.
What about you?

**Brain Trainer
Activity 3**
Go to page 59

Reading

1 Look quickly at Ella's blog and the photos. What do you think her blog is about?

  1 Her family.
  2 A visit to a museum.
  3 Her favorite movies.

2 Read and check your answer to Exercise 1.

3 Match each paragraph (1–4) to a photo (a–d).

4 Read Ella's blog again. Are the statements true (T) or false (F)?
1.18

  1 Leo is wearing science fiction makeup. *F*
  2 Annika and Max are in a science fiction movie.
  3 Ella likes Wallace and Gromit.
  4 Jack and his friends are watching a historical movie.
  5 The Charlie Chaplin movie has special effects.

5 What about you? In pairs, ask and answer.

  1 How often do you watch movies?
  2 When do you go to the movies?
  3 What is your favorite movie?
  4 Who is your favorite actor?
  5 Do you like movies with special effects?

> When do you watch movies?

> I usually watch movies on the weekend.

Ella's Blog

> Hi. I'm Ella. Welcome to my blog.

Places to visit in my town: The Film Museum

Do you like watching westerns, musicals, documentaries or action movies? Do you think science fiction and fantasy movies are cool? Then I know just the place for you, the Film Museum in my town. You can watch movies, act in a movie or make your own five-minute movies! Here are photos from my last visit with my friends.

1 What are Annika, Max and Dan doing in this photo? They're dancing in the musical *Fame*, and they're having a lot of fun! Max is singing, too, but he isn't a very good singer!

2 Look at Leo. He's wearing horror movie makeup in this photo. He isn't smiling. He looks serious and really scary!

3 Look at Jack in this photo. He's sitting in one of the museum's movie theater seats, and he's eating popcorn. He's watching a silent movie with our friends. It's a black-and-white Charlie Chaplin comedy. It's great, but it doesn't have any dialogue or special effects. (I'm not joking!)

4 We're making an animation here. It's taking a long time! I'm a big Wallace and Gromit fan. I love *The Wrong Trousers*. It's really funny!

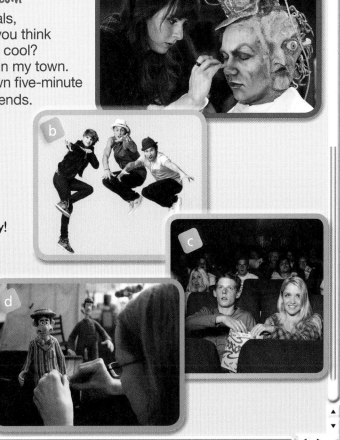

Grammar • Present continuous

Affirmative		
I	'm (am) making	
He/She/It	's (is) making	a movie.
You/We/They	're (are) making	

Negative		
I	'm not (am not) making	
He/She/It	isn't (is not) making	a movie.
You/We/They	aren't (are not) making	

Questions and short answers	
Am I making a movie?	Yes, I am. No, I'm not.
Is he/she/it making a movie?	Yes, he/she/it is. No, he/she/it isn't.
Are you/we/they making a movie?	Yes, you/we/they are. No, you/we/they aren't.

Wh questions
What am I doing? What is he/she/it doing? What are you/we/they doing?

Grammar reference page 110

Watch Out!

wait → waiting
get → getting
make → making

1 Study the grammar table. Choose the correct options to complete the rules.

  1 We use the Present continuous to talk about actions *in progress / in the past.*

  2 We make the Present continuous with the Present simple of *be / has* + verb + the *-ing* form of the verb.

2 What are the *-ing* forms of these verbs?

  1 begin *beginning*   7 run
  2 carry   8 sit
  3 dance   9 smile
  4 joke   10 stop
  5 look   11 study
  6 play   12 take

3 Complete the sentences and questions with the verbs in the Present continuous.

  1 They *are not waiting* (not wait) outside the movie theater. They *are sitting* (sit) inside it.
  2 Daniel .... (not eat) candy. He .... (eat) popcorn.
  3 We .... (not visit) the Film Museum. We .... (buy) tickets at the movie theater.
  4 You .... (not finish) your homework. You .... (watch) a horror movie on TV.
  5 Mark .... (not watch) the documentary. He .... (call) a friend.
  6 .... Lily .... (make) an animation? Yes, ...
  7 What .... Mark and Paul .... (watch) at the movies?

4 Complete the text with the Present continuous. Then listen and check.
1.19

It's nine o'clock and Paul [1] *is waiting* (wait) outside the movie theater for Sam and Kate. A horror movie, *The Beasts*, is playing, starting at 9:15. Paul is trying to call his friends, but they [2] .... (not answer). It [3] .... (rain) and it's dark. Paul isn't happy. Suddenly there's a noise behind him. Who [4] .... (run) down the street? It isn't the beasts. It's Kate and Sam! "Sorry we're late," says Kate.

5 Write questions and answers about Exercise 4.

  1 it / raining / Is / ?
    Is it raining? Yes, it is.
  2 Kate / waiting / outside the movie theater / Is / ?
  3 on the phone / talking / Is / Paul / ?
  4 Kate and Sam / Are / running / ?

6 What about you? What are these people doing at the moment? Use your imagination!

  • your friends and family
  • your favorite movie stars or pop stars

Vocabulary • Adjectives

1 **Look at the pictures and these words.**
1.20 **Listen and repeat.**

annoying	awesome	boring	exciting
expensive	funny	romantic	sad
scary	tasty	terrible	weird

Word list page 43
Workbook page 117

It's annoying.

It's awesome!

It's boring.

It's exciting!

It's expensive.

It's funny!

It's romantic.

It's sad.

It's scary!

It's tasty.

It's terrible.

It's weird!

2 **Copy the table and put the adjectives from Exercise 1 in the correct column.**

Positive	Negative	Can be both
awesome		

3 **Choose the correct options.**

1 *The Ring* is a horror movie. It's very *scary / romantic*.
2 The songs in the musical are good, but the actors are *terrible / sad*.
3 I like documentaries. They're *awesome / boring*.
4 It's a good action movie. It's *annoying / exciting*.
5 Ben Stiller is often in comedies. He's a *scary / funny* actor.
6 Try the popcorn. It's really *tasty / expensive*!

4 **Complete the sentences with the words in Exercise 1.**

1 All my friends are crying because the movie is very *sad*.
2 This movie is a comedy, but it's not funny. It's .... .
3 Johnny Depp is a really good actor. I think he's .... !
4 You can pay $17.50 for movie tickets in Los Angeles. That's .... !
5 I don't understand this movie at all. It's .... .
6 My friend always arrives late. It's .... .

Pronunciation
Word stress in adjectives

5a **Listen and repeat the adjectives.**
1.21 <u>bor</u>ing   ex<u>ci</u>ting

b **Listen. Where is the stress on the adjective?**
1.22
1 expensive
2 funny
3 romantic
4 terrible
5 scary
6 tasty
7 annoying
8 awesome

c **Listen and repeat.**
1.22

6 **Write your own examples for the words in Exercise 1. Read your sentences to a partner.**

I love this movie. It's funny!

Brain Trainer Activity 4
Go to page 59

Chatroom Suggestions

Speaking and Listening

1 Listen and read the conversation. What type of
1.23 movie do they like? Copy and complete the table.

	Jody	Nadia	Zak
Romantic			
Historical			
Comedy			

2 Listen and read again. Answer the questions.
1.23
1 What movie does Jody suggest?
  Jane Eyre.
2 Why is Nadia surprised?
3 Does Zak want to see *Jane Eyre*?
  Why?/Why not?
4 Which type of movie does Jody like?
5 What does Nadia suggest?
6 What does Zak think of Nadia's idea?

3 Act out the conversation in groups of three.

Jody Hi, Nadia. Hi, Zak. Why don't we go to the movies?

Nadia Hi, Jody. That's a good idea. Are there any good movies playing?

Jody What about *Jane Eyre*?

Nadia But that's a historical movie, and you never see historical movies.

Jody Well, I want to see this one! I'm reading the book at the moment, and it's so sad and romantic!

Nadia Great! I love historical movies. What about you, Zak?

Zak No way! I think historical movies are silly, and Carlos hates them, too. Let's see a comedy. What about *Zookeeper*?

Jody No, thanks! I don't like comedies … They're stupid. I like romantic movies.

Nadia I have an idea. Jody and I can see *Jane Eyre*, and you and Carlos can see *Zookeeper*.

Zak Great! I'm in!

Say it in your language …
No way!
I'm in!

4 Look back at the conversation. Who says what?

1 Why don't we go to the movies? *Jody*
2 That's a good idea.
3 What about *Jane Eyre*?
4 Great!
5 No way!
6 Let's see a comedy.

5 Read the phrases for making and responding to suggestions.

Making suggestions	Responding
Let's …	Great!
Why don't we … ?	That's a good idea. I'm in!
What about … ? How about . . . ?	No, thanks! No way!

6 Listen to the conversation. Act out the conversation
1.24 in pairs.

Carlos Why don't we see [1] *Night at the Museum 2*? It's [2] funny.
Zak No, thanks! I don't like [3] Ben Stiller.
Carlos How about watching [4] *Star Trek*? The [5] special effects are [6] great.
Zak I'm in! I love [7] science fiction movies. Let's watch it at my house.
Carlos Good idea.

7 Work in pairs. Replace the words in purple in Exercise 6. Use these words and/or your own ideas. Act out the conversation.

Why don't we watch *Avatar*? It's very exciting.

No, thanks!

1 *Twilight* / *Avatar* / *One Day*
2 great / fun / scary / romantic / exciting
3 Robert Pattinson / Zoe Saldana / Anne Hathaway
4 *Mamma Mia* / *Kung Fu Panda* / *Karate Kid*
5 songs / actors / costumes / fight scenes
6 fantastic / amazing / cool / awesome
7 musicals / westerns / comedies / horror movies

Grammar • Present simple and Present continuous

Present simple	Present continuous
Jody never watches historical movies.	She's reading *Jane Eyre* at the moment.

Grammar reference page 110

1 Study the grammar table. Complete the rules with *continuous* or *simple*.

1 We use the Present … for actions that are in progress now.
2 We use the Present … for habits, routines or things that are always true.

2 Choose the correct options.

1 Luke usually *watches* / *is watching* horror movies, but now he *watches* / *'s watching* a comedy.
2 Lisa usually *goes* / *is going* to her photography class on Saturdays, but this Saturday she *works* / *is working* at her mom's café.
3 Beth often *goes* / *is going* to the café after school, but she *watches* / *is watching* a soccer game at the moment.

3 Look at the table. What do the people usually do? What are they doing at the moment?

Sally usually takes photographs, but at the moment she is doing a school project.

	usually	at the moment
Sally	take photographs	do / school project
Norah	play soccer	watch / TV
Sam and Ben	go / to a dance class	sleep

4 Imagine it's Monday, but it's a holiday. Say what you usually do and what you are doing today.

On Monday, I usually …, but today I …

go / to school	go / to the beach
read / my textbooks	read / a magazine
listen / to my teachers	listen / to the radio
sit / at my desk	sit / in the sun

Reading

1 Look quickly at the text. What kind of text do you think it is?

1 A movie review.
2 A newspaper article.
3 An interview in a magazine.

My Movies: **EXTRA SPECIAL**

This week we're on the movie set of *Twilight*, but we're not talking to Robert Pattinson. We're interviewing student Tom Dalton. Tom has an amazing summer job this year!

WHAT'S YOUR SUMMER JOB, TOM?
I'm a movie extra. It's fun, but I don't speak. I'm in the background.

YOU'RE NOT THE STAR OF THE MOVIE, THEN?
No, I'm not, but extras are important. They help to make the movie realistic.

WHAT'S THE MOVIE ABOUT?
It's about vampires, but it's not scary. It's romantic.

IS THAT A VAMPIRE COSTUME?
Yes, it is. We're all wearing black clothes and white makeup today.

AND WHAT'S HAPPENING AT THE MOMENT?
They're doing a scene in the castle of the Volturi. The director is filming the ending and it's very exciting.

IS THE ENDING HAPPY OR SAD?
I can't tell you. It's a secret!

IS IT EXCITING WORK?
Yes, it is usually exciting, but at the moment it's boring because we're waiting for an actor. He's not here!

ARE THERE ANY FAMOUS ACTORS ON THE MOVIE SET TODAY?
Well, there's Robert Pattinson. He's Edward Cullen, the main character. But we can't talk to him and we can't take pictures of him.

WHY NOT? DOES HE BITE?
No, he doesn't, but we can't talk to him because he's very busy!

THANKS, TOM. GOOD LUCK!

Key Words

extra	background	star
scene	director	character

2 Read and check your answer to Exercise 1.

3 Read the text. Are the statements true (T), false (F) or don't know (DK)?
1.25

1 Tom has an amazing job this summer. *T*
2 He talks in the movie.
3 Tom is one of the stars.
4 The movie is scary.
5 The movie has a happy ending.
6 Tom's job is usually boring.

4 Read the interview again. Answer the questions.
1.25

1 Why are extras important in a movie?
   They help make the movie realistic.
2 What is Tom wearing today?
3 Where does the ending of the movie happen?
4 Why is Tom's job boring at the moment?
5 Who is the star? What part does he play?
6 Why can't Tom talk to him?

Listening

1 Read the advertisement. Listen to four people.
1.26 Which speakers want to be an extra?

i movie

LOOKING FOR EXTRAS!
iMovie is making a new action movie, and we're looking for extras NOW!

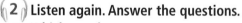

2 Listen again. Answer the questions.
1.26 Which speaker:

1 talks about his/her favorite actor?
2 is shopping?
3 sends a text message to his/her friends?
4 wants free movie tickets?

Writing • A movie review

1 Read the Writing File.

> **Writing File** Linking words
>
> - **Addition**
>   We can't talk to him, and we can't take pictures of him.
> - **Contrast**
>   The movie is about vampires, but it's not scary.
> - **Reason**
>   We can't talk to him because he's busy.

2 Read Claire's movie review. Find *and, but* and *because*.

My Favorite Movie

My favorite movie is *Fame*. I have the DVD, and I often watch it with my sister because we love musicals! My mom sometimes watches it with us, but my dad never watches it. He hates musicals!

Fame is about a group of American students at the School for Performing Arts in New York. The students at the school are actors, and they also sing and dance. There are a lot of songs. My dad thinks they're boring, but I think they're great.

I like *Fame* because the characters in the movie are really interesting. The main characters of the movie are Denise Dupree and Victor Tavares.

I like Denise. She plays a romantic character, but she's also very funny in *Fame*.

In my opinion, *Fame* is great because the story and the characters are fantastic, and the songs are amazing! ★ ★ ★

3 Choose the correct options.

1 Sarah likes horror movies, *and / because* she often watches action movies.
2 Louise doesn't like documentaries, *and / but* she likes animations.
3 Mark enjoys comedies, *and / but* he doesn't tell jokes.
4 Jeremy loves science fiction movies, *because / and* they're exciting.
5 My parents don't watch musicals, *but / because* they think they're boring.

4 Read Claire's movie review again. Answer the questions.

1 What type of movie is *Fame*? *A musical*
2 What is it about?
3 Who is Claire's favorite character?
4 Why does she like this movie?

5 Think about your favorite movie. Answer the questions. Take notes.

1 What is your favorite movie?
2 What type of movie is it?
3 What is the movie about?
4 Who is your favorite character?
5 What's your opinion of the movie?

6 Write a review of your favorite movie. Use "My movie review" and your notes from Exercise 5.

> My movie review ⊗
>
> 1 Name and type of movie
>   *My favorite movie is* (name) .... .
>   *It's a(n)* (type of movie) .... .
> 2 Description of story
>   *.... is about* ....
> 3 Why I like the movie
>   *I like .... because* .... .
>   *My favorite character is .... because* .... .
> 4 Conclusion
>   *In my opinion, ... is a .... movie.*

> **Remember!**
> Use linking words: *and, because, but.*
> Use the vocabulary in this unit.
> Check your grammar, spelling and punctuation.

Refresh Your Memory!

Grammar • Review

1 Complete the sentences with these verbs in the Present continuous.

> do ~~send~~ sing study talk watch

1 I'm sending a text message to my friend right now.
2 Mikey and Nick .... TV at the moment.
3 My mom .... on the phone now.
4 Ella .... in the musical.
5 We .... English today.
6 They .... their homework.

2 Make the sentences in Exercise 1 negative.

1 I'm not sending a text message to my friend right now.

3 Complete the Present continuous questions. Then match each question to an answer.

1 Are you watching (watch) a DVD?
  e Yes, we are.
2 .... the movie .... (start) now?
3 .... she .... (make) a movie?
4 .... they .... (sit) at the back of the movie theater?
5 .... you .... (take) a photograph?

a Yes, they are.
b No, I'm not.
c No, it isn't.
d Yes, she is.
e Yes, we are.

4 Complete the text with the Present simple or Present continuous form of the verbs.

Joe [1] usually watches (usually / watch) science fiction movies, but today he [2] .... (watch) Black Wolf with his sisters, Daisy and Holly. It's a horror movie, but it's a comedy, too. Joe [3] .... (not like) horror movies, but Daisy and Holly [4] .... (always / enjoy) them. The movie is very funny. At the moment, a boy in the movie [5] .... (look) for his family. He's sad, but Joe [6] .... (laugh). Why is he doing that? Because Daisy [7] .... (cry). Daisy and Holly [8] .... (often / cry) at sad scenes in movies!

Vocabulary • Review

5 Complete the adjectives.

1 "I enjoy funny movies with a lot of jokes."
2 "I love sc_r_ movies."
3 "I enjoy watching _xc_t_ng movies about the future!"
4 "My favorite movies are often _xp_ns_v_, with special effects."
5 "I think movies about real life are t_rr_bl_."
6 "I think movies about people from long ago are _w_s_m_."
7 "Most cartoons are really _nn_y_ng."
8 "Cowboy movies are b_r_ng."
9 "Science fiction movies are really w_ _rd. I like movies about Japanese fighters."
10 "War movies are very s_d. I like songs in movies."

6 Match the movie types to the sentences in Exercise 5.

1 action movies *4*   6 animations
2 comedies   7 documentaries
3 martial arts movies   8 historical movies
4 horror movies   9 westerns
5 musicals   10 science fiction movies

Speaking • Review

7 Complete the conversation with these words. Then listen and check.
1.27

> good ~~let's~~ no no what why

James   [1] Let's have popcorn.
Lily   [2] ..., thanks. I don't like popcorn.
James   [3] .... don't we have an ice cream?
Lily   [4] .... way! It's too cold for that!
James   OK. [5] .... about chips?
Lily   [6] .... idea!

Dictation

8 Listen and write in your notebook.
1.28

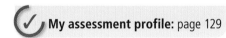

✓ **My assessment profile:** page 129

Kishan Shrikanth's Profile

Age	**Home country**
14 years old	India

My favorite …

movies	horror, action
actors	Keanu Reeves, Tom Cruise
director	Steven Spielberg
things	sports and movies!

Reading

1 Read Kishan's profile. Are the statements true (T) or false (F)?

1 Kishan comes from India. *T*
2 Kishan hates horror movies.
3 Kishan's two favorite things are reading and movies.

2 Read the article. Answer the questions.

1.29

1 Why is Kishan famous?
Because he's an Indian movie director.
2 What is *Care of Footpath* about?
3 Where do street children live?
4 Why is it difficult for them to change their lives?
5 What does Slummu want to do?
6 Who is *Care of Footpath* for?
7 What is the message of the movie?
8 What is Kishan doing at the moment?

  # Kishan's Movie

Kishan Shrikanth is 14 years old. He lives in India, and he's very famous there. Why? Because he's a movie director! His new movie is in theaters in India this year. It's called *Care of Footpath.*

Care of Footpath is very different from other Bollywood movies. It isn't a comedy or a musical. It's the story of a young street child in Bangalore. Street children in India are very poor. They live on the streets of big cities. Their lives are very hard. They don't go to school, and it's difficult for them to change their lives.

Care of Footpath is very sad in the beginning, but it has a happy ending. The main character is named Slummu. Slummu has a dream. He wants to go to school and study, but how? At the end of the movie, Slummu's dream comes true!

Kishan wants to help street children in India and other countries. He says *Care of Footpath* is for street children all over the world. The message of the movie is "nothing is impossible." At the moment, Kishan is making another movie. It's about a group of Indian teenagers and their different problems!

Class discussion

1 Are there problems like this in your country?
2 Do all the children in your country go to school?
3 What different problems do teenagers have in your country?

3 Past Lives

Vocabulary • History

1 Listen and repeat. Then match ten of these words to the picture.
1.30

army	castle 1	century	die	dungeon	kill	king	knight
plague	prisoner	queen	servant	soldier	sword	war	

2 Which words in Exercise 1 are not in the picture?
Which of these words means …

1 to stop living? *die*
2 to make a person or animal die?
3 a terrible disease?
4 a hundred years?
5 a time of fighting between countries?

3 Complete the sentences with the words in
Exercise 1.

1 The *king* and .... live in a big castle.
2 A .... is a disease that kills a lot of people.
3 When there is a war, many people .... .
4 The .... has 10,000 soldiers.
5 The .... in the castle cook and clean.
6 This castle is from the fourteenth .... .
7 The dungeon is for .... .

4 In pairs, talk about the things from history
you like and don't like.

> I like learning about kings.
> What about you?

> I like learning about them, but
> I don't like reading about wars.

**Brain Trainer
Activity 3**
Go to page 60

Reading

1 Look at the text quickly. Is it:

1 from an encyclopedia?
2 from a short story?
3 an advertisement for a tourist attraction?

2 Read and check your answer to Exercise 1.

3 Read the text again. Are the statements true (T) or false (F)?

1.31

1 At the London Dungeon you can only learn about two horrible events. *F*
2 Rats carried the plague from London to the ships.
3 In 1665 many rich people left London because they didn't want to die.
4 The plague killed about 80,000 people in London.
5 The Great Fire of London started in the same year as the Great Plague.
6 During the fire there were many victims in London.
7 You can meet horrible people from history in the Labyrinth.

4 What about you? Think of a tourist attraction in your country. In pairs, ask and answer.

1 What is it?
2 Where is it?
3 What can you do there?

> St. George's Castle is a famous tourist attraction in Portugal.

> Where is it?

> It's in Lisbon.

The London Dungeon

What can you do at The London Dungeon?

Come and see London at the time of the Great Plague and the Great Fire! Learn about other horrible events in English history!

The Great Plague

In the fourteenth century a terrible plague killed many thousands of people in England. The plague came and went many times in the next three hundred years. Then, in 1665, rats from ships carried the disease to London again. King Charles II and many rich people went to the country to escape the plague, but poor people didn't leave the city. They stayed, and about 80,000 people died.

The Great Fire of London

After the Great Plague, there was a very big fire in London. On September 2, 1666, a fire started at the bakery of Thomas Farriner in Pudding Lane. Farriner and his family escaped, but their servant died in the fire. The fire started in this poor part of the city and then burned the old City of London, including 13,500 houses, 87 churches and St. Paul's Cathedral. The fire was terrible, but there were not many victims, and only six people died. Is this really true, or did more people die? It's a mystery!

Other things to do

Go for a boat ride in the dark, see the ghosts in the Labyrinth of the Lost Souls, or meet horrible people from history!

Grammar • Past simple

To be Affirmative		
I/He/She/It	was	old.
You/We/They	were	

To be Negative		
I/He/She/It	wasn't (was not)	old.
You/We/They	weren't (were not)	

To be: Questions and short answers	
Was I/he/she/it old?	Yes, I/he/she/it was.
	No, I/he/she/it wasn't.
Were you/we/they old?	Yes, you/we/they were.
	No, you/we/they weren't.

Regular verbs: affirmative and negative		
I/You/He/She/It/We/They	stayed	in London.
I/You/He/She/It/We/They	didn't (did not) stay	in London.

Irregular verbs: affirmative and negative		
I/You/He/She/It/We/They	left	the city.
I/You/He/She/It/We/They	didn't (did not) leave	the city.

Time expressions		
yesterday	yesterday evening	last year
three years ago	in 1666	

Grammar reference page 112

Watch Out!

cook → cooked   dance → danced
stop → stopped   hurry → hurried

1 Study the grammar table. Choose the correct options to complete the rules.

1 The past forms of *regular / irregular* verbs end in -*ed*.
2 The past forms of *regular / irregular* verbs are all different. It is important to learn them.

2 What is the Past simple form of these verbs?

1 play *played*	7 do	13 see
2 go	8 carry	14 like
3 start	9 eat	15 write
4 read	10 give	16 take
5 clean	11 listen	17 come
6 drink	12 hear	18 sit

3 Complete the sentences with the Past simple.

1 She *did* (do) her history homework last night.
2 The soldiers .... (fight) in the war.
3 The young man .... (become) a knight.
4 I .... (have) a terrible day yesterday.
5 They .... (study) for a test last night.
6 You .... (make) a big mistake!

4 Complete the sentences with these words.

give	learn	leave	~~play~~	read	watch

1 We *played* tennis on Saturday.
2 Luke and Jason .... a horror movie last night.
3 He .... me a present for my birthday.
4 I .... a text about ancient Rome. I .... about Julius Caesar.
5 You .... school early yesterday.

Pronunciation Verb endings: /t/, /d/, /ɪd/

5a Listen and repeat the sentences.
1.32
1 /t/:   We liked the castle.
2 /d/:   He traveled to London.
3 /ɪd/:   The fire started there.

b Listen. Copy the table and put the verbs in the
1.33 correct column.

~~asked~~	died	ended	escaped	happened
lived	visited	wanted	watched	

/t/	/d/	/ɪd/
asked		

c Listen, check and repeat.
1.34

6 Rewrite the sentences in the negative form.

1 We went to London on the weekend.
They didn't go to London on the weekend.
2 They visited a castle in Scotland. I .... .
3 He read a story about a famous knight. She .... .
4 I saw a sword at the museum. You .... .
5 The museum opened at ten. The restaurant .... .
6 We had a history test last week. They .... .
7 I was in London two weeks ago. He .... .

7 Complete the email with the Past simple form of these verbs.

~~arrive~~	be	go	have	learn
not buy	not come	not feel	not have	see
stay	visit			

New Message ⊗

Hi Barbara!
Well, we ¹ *arrived* in London ten days ago. Last Friday Dad and I ² .... to the Tower of London. It ³ .... fantastic, and we ⁴ .... a lot about English history. Mom ⁵ .... with us because she ⁶ .... well. She ⁷ .... at the hotel.
Yesterday we ⁸ .... the Imperial War Museum. Then we ⁹ .... lunch at a fish-and-chip shop. In the afternoon we went shopping on Regent Street. I ¹⁰ .... some beautiful clothes. I ¹¹ .... them because I ¹² .... any money. Oh well! Next time.
See you soon,
Diana

Send

Add Attachments ⊗

8 What about you? What did you do last weekend? Write sentences.

On Saturday I didn't get up early. I got up at ten. I had breakfast, and then I met my friends downtown …

Vocabulary • Life events

1 Listen and repeat. Then match eight of these
1.35 words to the pictures.

be born *1*	die	fall in love
find a job	get married	go to college
graduate	have a baby	leave home
move	retire	start school

Word list page 43
Workbook page 118

2 Which words in Exercise 1 are not in the pictures?

3 Choose the correct options. Then listen and check.
1.36
Megan Davies ¹ *was / had* born in 1953.
She ² *started / left* school when she was five and ³ *started / left* school when she was eighteen.
After school, she ⁴ *went / retired* to college.
She ⁵ *retired / graduated* in 1974. She ⁶ *got / left* home when she ⁷ *met / found* a job. She met John and ⁸ *started / fell* in love with him.
They ⁹ *got / had* married two months later.
Megan ¹⁰ *had / was* a baby in 1977. After two years, Megan and John ¹¹ *moved / left*. Megan ¹² *retired / graduated* when she was 60.

Brain Trainer
Activity 4
Go to page 60

Chatroom Reasoning

Speaking and Listening

1 **Look at the photo. Answer the questions.**

1 Where do you think the four friends are?
2 What are they doing there?
3 What's wrong with Nadia?

2 **Listen and read the conversation. Check your answers.**
1.37

3 **Listen and read again. Answer the questions.**
1.37
1 Why does Zak say "Say 'Cheese'"?
Because he wants to take a photo.
2 Where does Jody want to go?
3 Why does she want to go there?
4 Why doesn't Nadia want to go?
5 Who killed the young princes in the Tower?
6 What is a raven?
7 What can the ravens do?

4 **Act out the conversation in groups of five.**

Zak	OK, guys. I want to take a photo. Say "Cheese"!
Nadia	No, Zak. I'm tired. And my feet hurt!
Jody	Forget the photo. Let's visit the Bloody Tower.
Nadia	Why?
Jody	Because there are ghosts in it!
Nadia	Then I don't want to see it.
Jody	Don't be silly, Nadia. Why don't you want to see it?
Nadia	Because I'm scared of ghosts.
Mr. Jones	Well, I'm not sure there are ghosts, but King Richard III killed two young princes there.
Raven	Good morning!
Zak	Did you hear that?!
Carlos	Yes, I did. It was that bird.
Mr. Jones	Yes, that's a raven. The ravens at the Tower of London are famous. They watch over the Tower.
Jody	And they can talk!

Say it in your language …
Say "Cheese"!
Don't be silly.

5 Look back at the conversation. Complete the sentences.

1 Say *"Cheese"*!
2 .... there are ghosts in it!
3 I .... want to see it.
4 Don't .... silly.
5 .... don't you want to see it?
6 .... I'm scared of ghosts.

6 Read the phrases for asking for and giving reasons.

Asking for a reason	Giving a reason
Why?/Why not?	Because ...
Why do/don't you want to ... ?	

7 Listen to the conversations. Act out the
1.38 conversations in pairs.

Zak Let's go to ¹ the War Museum.
Nadia Why?
Zak Because ² it's interesting.
Nadia ³ That's a good idea.

Zak I want to go to ¹ the London Dungeon.
Nadia Why do you want to go there?
Zak Because ² it's scary.
Nadia ³ No way!

8 Work in pairs. Replace the words in purple in Exercise 7. Use these words and/or your own ideas. Act out the conversations.

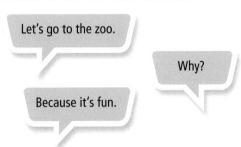

1 the castle / zoo / park / stores

2 (it's/they're) interesting / exciting / boring / fun / scary / terrible

3 That's a good idea. / No way! / No, thanks. / OK. / All right.

Grammar • Past simple: questions and short answers

Regular verbs: questions and short answers
Did I/you/he/she/it/we/they stay in London?
Yes, I/you/he/she/it/we/they did.
No, I/you/he/she/it/we/they didn't (did not).

Irregular verbs: questions and short answers
Did I/you/he/she/it/we/they leave the city?
Yes, I/you/he/she/it/we/they did.
No, I/you/he/she/it/we/they didn't (did not).

Wh questions
Where did you stay?   When did they leave?

Grammar reference page 112

1 Study the grammar table. Choose the correct options to complete the rules.

1 In Past simple questions, we use *did + the infinitive / the Past simple form of the verb*.
2 In Past simple short answers, we *use / don't use* the verb after *did* and *didn't*.

2 Make questions with the Past simple.

1 I took a photo of the castle. (you)
   Did you take a photo of the castle?
2 He studied his history notes. (she)
3 We saw a ghost in the Tower. (they)
4 You had lunch at one o'clock. (he)
5 She got a good grade on the test. (you)
6 They visited the Dungeon. (he)

3 Make questions with the words in columns A and B.

Did you visit your grandparents yesterday?

A	B
visit your grandparents	on the weekend
have English class	last night
meet your friends	last week
walk to school	this morning
watch TV	yesterday

4 In pairs, ask and answer the questions in Exercise 3.

Did you visit your grandparents yesterday?

Yes, I did.

Reading

1 **Look at the photo. Answer the questions.**

1 Who is this man?
2 Why is he famous?
3 What do you know about him?

William Shakespeare (1564–1616)

William Shakespeare was born in Stratford-upon-Avon, England, in 1564. He probably went to school, but he didn't go to college. When he was eighteen, William married Anne Hathaway. They had a son named Hamnet and two daughters, Susanna and Judith. Hamnet died of the plague when he was eleven.

In 1585, Shakespeare left his family in Stratford and went to London. There he started a career as an actor, a writer and the owner of a theater with some other actors. He retired in 1613 and died three years later.

William Shakespeare wrote about thirty-eight plays: comedies (e.g., *A Midsummer Night's Dream*), tragedies (e.g., *Romeo and Juliet*) and historical plays (e.g., *Richard III*).

Some people think that Shakespeare didn't write his plays. They believe that another mystery person wrote them. Why? Because in the sixteenth century, writers were often rich and went to college. They usually traveled and spoke different languages. Shakespeare didn't come from a rich family or study at a college, and he stayed in England all his life. Most people believe Shakespeare was the author of the plays, but there are questions about his life: Why did he marry Anne Hathaway? Why did he move to London? Why did he retire? How did he die?

Shakespeare's plays are famous all over the world, but his life has many mysteries.

Key Words

career	owner	play
tragedy	mystery	author

2 **Read and check your answers to Exercise 1.**

3 1.39 **Read the text again. Complete the sentences with the correct years or numbers.**

1 Shakespeare was born in *1564.*
2 He got married in ..... .
3 He had .... children.
4 Shakespeare moved to London when he was .... years old.
5 He stopped writing in ..... .
6 He died in ..... .
7 He wrote .... plays.

4 1.39 **Read the text again. Answer the questions.**

1 Where was Shakespeare born?
  He was born in Stratford-upon-Avon, England.
2 Did he go to college?
3 What was his wife's name?
4 Why did his son die?
5 Did Shakespeare's family go with him to London?
6 What did Shakespeare do in London?
7 What kinds of plays did Shakespeare write?
8 Why do some people think that Shakespeare didn't write his plays?

Listening

1 1.40 **Read the questions. Guess the correct answers. Listen and check.**

1 How old was Anne Hathaway when she got married?
  a sixteen   b twenty-two   c twenty-six
2 How many wives did Philip II of Spain have?
  a two   b three   c four
3 The father of the young princes in the Tower was…
  a Richard III.   b Henry VI.   c Edward IV.

2 1.40 **Listen again. Complete the sentences.**

1 Shakespeare and Anne Hathaway got married on the 27th or 28th of ..... .
2 Mary and Philip got married in ..... .
3 Mary of .... was Philip II's second wife.
4 The names of the two princes in the Tower were .... and ..... .
5 Peter scores .... out of ..... .

Writing • A biography

1 Read the Writing File.

2 Match the paragraphs (A–C) to the correct categories (1–3).
1 Name, date of birth, place of birth.
2 Education and work.
3 Other important information.

Sofonisba Anguissola

A Sofonisba was famous because she was a great painter, and she painted important people. You can see a painting of Philip II by her in the Prado Museum in Madrid today. She also helped other women in the sixteenth century to become artists. She died in 1625.

B Sofonisba Anguissola was born in 1532 in Lombardy in the north of Italy.

C She studied painting with four of her sisters in Italy. She met Michelangelo in Rome in 1554, and he gave her some ideas for her paintings. In 1559, Sofonisba left Italy and moved to Spain. She lived and worked there in the palace of King Philip II. She painted many beautiful pictures at this time and became the art teacher of Philip's third wife, Elizabeth of Valois.

3 Read the biography of Sofonisba again. Answer the questions.
1 When was Sofonisba born?
   She was born in 1532.
2 Where was she born?
3 Who did she study painting with?
4 Where did she study painting?
5 Who gave her ideas for her paintings?
6 When did she leave Italy?
7 Where did she live in Spain?
8 Who was Elizabeth of Valois?
9 Why did Sofonisba become famous?
10 Where can you see her painting of Philip II today?

4 Think of a famous person from your country. Find information about him/her and take notes about the following:
1 his/her name, date of birth and place of birth
2 his/her education and work
3 other important information about him/her

5 Write a biography of your famous person. Use "My biography of …" and your notes from Exercise 4.

My biography of …
1 Name, date of birth, place of birth
   …. was born in …. in …. .
2 Education and work
   When she/he was …. she/he …. .Then …. .
3 Other important information
   …. died in …. .

Remember!
- Organize your biography in three sections.
- Use the vocabulary in this unit.
- Check your grammar, spelling and punctuation.

Refresh Your Memory!

Grammar • Review

1 Copy and complete the table with these verbs in the Past simple form.

| become | do | die | have | leave |
| live | read | see | stay | study |

Regular	Irregular
	became

2 Complete the sentences with the Past simple form of the verb *to be*.

1 She *wasn't* tall; she was short.
2 What .... Shakespeare's first name?
3 .... there any people in the castle?
4 It .... an interesting place.
5 The buildings .... old; they were new.

3 Choose the correct answer.

1 When .... she born?
  a did   b does   c *was*
2 I didn't .... to the museum on the weekend.
  a go   b went   c going
3 We .... a movie about London yesterday.
  a see   b saw   c did see
4 They .... like the Tower of London.
  a not   b doesn't   c didn't
5 She .... to school by bus yesterday.
  a did go   b went   c go
6 "Did you learn about the kings and queens of England?" "Yes, we .... "
  a did   b did go   c went
7 How many plays .... ?
  a Shakespeare wrote
  b wrote Shakespeare
  c did Shakespeare write
8 Shakespeare died hundreds of years .... .
  a ago   b last   c before

Vocabulary • Review

4 Complete the sentences with these words.

| castle | ~~century~~ | killed | prisoners |
| servants | sword | wars | |

1 Jeanne d'Arc lived in the fifteenth *century*.
2 Thousands of soldiers died in the .... between France and England.
3 The king put the .... in the dungeon.
4 King Charles VII of France lived in the .... of Chinon.
5 They were rich, and their .... cooked and cleaned the house for them.
6 The knight had a .... and a white horse.
7 The plague .... many people.

5 Complete the text with these words.

| ~~born~~ | got | graduated | had | left | moved |

Barack Obama was ¹*born* in Honolulu, Hawaii, in 1961. He went to school in Indonesia and Hawaii. When he ² .... school, he studied law in New York. He ³ .... from law school in 1983. He and Michelle Robinson ⁴ .... married in 1992. They ⁵ .... their first child in 1998. When Barack Obama became president of the United States in 2009, he and his family ⁶ .... into the White House in Washington, DC.

Speaking • Review

6 Put the conversation in the correct order, 1–6. Then listen and check.
1.41

  .1. Let's go to the old castle today.
  .... Because I like castles. They're really cool!
  .... Why not?
  .... Why?
  .... Because castles are boring!
  .... No, thanks. I don't want to go.

Dictation

7 Listen and write in your notebook.
1.42

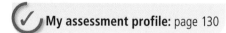

✓ **My assessment profile:** page 130

Ancient Civilizations

1 **Ancient Egypt** was a civilization in North Africa. The Nile River ran through ancient Egypt. Two separate kingdoms developed along the Nile River—the kingdom in Upper Egypt and the kingdom in Lower Egypt. In 3200 BC, the pharaoh of the north conquered the south, and Egypt became one country. The pharaoh's name was King Narmer, or Menes.

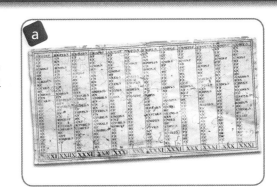

2 The **Roman Empire** began in Italy in 27 BC. It was small at first, but it became very big. In the end, North Africa, Spain, France, Germany and England were all part of it. The Romans play an important part in our lives today. Many of the things we do or have are from the Romans. The Romans spoke and wrote in Latin, and many of our words come from Latin words. Our calendar, for example, started with Julius Caesar, a Roman ruler.

3 The **Aztec** people were from central Mexico. From the 13th century, the Valley of Mexico was the center of the Aztec civilization. In AD 1325, the Aztecs lived in central Mexico City, a large, beautiful and powerful city, on a small island called Tenochtitlan. The ancient Aztecs believed in many gods and goddesses. Songs and poetry were also very important to them. There were poetry competitions at most of the Aztec festivals.

Reading

1 Read the text quickly. Match the pictures (a–c) to the paragraphs (1–3).

2 Read the text again. Write AE (Ancient Egypt), RE (Roman Empire) or AZ (Aztec) for sentences 1–6.
1.43

1 Menes was an ancient pharaoh. *AE*
2 Gods were very important to them.
3 Their empire began in 27 BC.
4 They spoke and wrote in Latin.
5 The Nile River was important to them.
6 Tenochtitlan was an island.

My History File

3 Take notes about a period of history. Think about:

- when it began/ended, important events (a brief history)
- facts about the culture, art, religion, etc.
- any other interesting information

4 Write a paragraph about the period of history. Add pictures. Use your notes from Exercise 3 to help you.

Grammar • Present simple

1 **Complete the sentences with the Present simple form of the verbs.**

1 I *play* (play) tennis with my friends on the weekend.
2 Sara .... (not read) sports magazines.
3 They .... (practice) ice skating at the ice skating rink every week.
4 You .... (not listen) to the same music as me.
5 He .... (finish) school at 3 p.m. every day.
6 We .... (not live) in downtown Chicago.
7 My brother .... (study) history in college.
8 We .... (watch) DVDs of our favorite action movies on Friday evenings.
9 Alice .... (wear) special clothes in her dance class.
10 I .... (not watch) sports on TV.

2 **Look at the table. Make questions and answers.**

	Jack	Leo	Alice
like football	✓	✗	✓
walk to school	✗	✓	✗
play tennis	✓	✓	✗

1 Jack and Alice / like / football?
   Do Jack and Alice like football?
   Yes, they do.
2 Jack and Alice / walk / to school?
3 Leo / walk / to school?
4 Jack and Leo / play / tennis?
5 Alice / play / tennis?

• Verb + -ing

3 **Make sentences.**

1 Ben / 😊😊 / play / football
   Ben loves playing football.
2 I / 😐 / watch / horror movies
3 your grandparents / 🙂 / go / for walks / ?
4 we / 😕 / study / for exams
5 you / 😞😞 / lose / games
6 Lara / 🙂 / read / music magazines

• Adverbs of frequency

4 **Make sentences.**

1 late / Sandra / goes / always / to bed
   Sandra always goes to bed late.
2 in the park / often / play / we / soccer / don't
3 usually / coffee / do / your parents / in the morning / drink / ?
4 I / score / never / for my team / goals
5 go / does / sometimes / to the gym / he / ?
6 hardly ever / Steve / goes / to the movies

• Present continuous

5 **Complete the text with the Present continuous form of these verbs.**

> have   read   not sit   ~~stay~~   watch   write

I ¹ *'m staying* with a great family here in Spain, and I ² .... a great time. At the moment I'm in the yard and I ³ .... this email to you on my new laptop. I ⁴ .... in the sun—it's very hot! My Spanish friend, Amelia, ⁵ .... a book, and her brother, Javi, ⁶ .... TV. Mr. and Mrs. Cruz are in the kitchen.

6 **Make Present continuous questions and answers.**

1 they / wait / for us / at the movie theater? ✓
   Are they waiting for us at the movie theater?
   Yes, they are.
2 what / you / do? (my homework)
3 he / listen / to his teacher? ✗
4 what / they / watch / on TV? (a western)
5 she / have / fun / at the museum? ✓
6 you and your friends / chat / on the phone? ✗

• Present continuous and Present simple

7 **Complete the texts with the Present simple or Present continuous form of the verbs in parentheses.**

I usually ¹ *walk* (walk) to school, but today it ² .... (rain) and my mom ³ .... (take) me to school in her car. What about you?

We ⁴ .... (usually / play) basketball on Saturdays, but today we're at the swimming pool. We ⁵ .... (watch) my little brother. He ⁶ .... (take) part in a swim meet.

• Past simple: affirmative and negative

8 Complete the sentences with the Past simple form of the verbs.

1 I *read* (read) a great book last week.
2 There .... (be) thousands of people at the concert.
3 Mom and Aunt Isabel .... (do) judo when they .... (be) in school.
4 They .... (not watch) the football game last night. They .... (watch) a DVD.
5 We .... (visit) the old castle yesterday.
6 I .... (wash) Dad's car last weekend.

9 Complete the text with the Past simple form of the verbs.

Martha Biggs is ninety years old today. She says: "I ¹ *didn't live* (not live) in a big city when I was young. I ² .... (live) in the country. My father ³ .... (die) when I was sixteen, and I ⁴ .... (not finish) school. I ⁵ .... (not go) to college, and I ⁶ .... (not travel) to other countries. I ⁷ .... (get) married when I was twenty-two. My husband and I ⁸ .... (not have) a lot of money, but we ⁹ .... (have) a good life."

• Past simple: questions

10 Complete the questions with the Past simple form of the verbs in parentheses.

1 I learned about the plague in history. What *did you learn* (you / learn) about?
2 She came here by car. How .... (they / come)?
3 We watched a martial arts movie. What type of movie .... (she / watch)?
4 My brother played in a soccer tournament. .... (your brother / play) in one, too?
5 I listened to my MP3 player this morning. .... (you / listen) to your MP3 player?
6 They saw their grandparents on Saturday. .... (you / see) your grandparents?

Speaking • Opinions

1 Complete the conversation with these words.

boring   do   ~~like~~   loved   think

A What did you think of the new *Transformers* movie?
B I didn't ¹ *like* it.
A Oh. I ² .... it. Shia LaBeouf was really good. ³ .... you like him?
B No, I don't. My favorite actor is Taylor Lautner.
A Did you ⁴ .... the story was good?
B No, I thought it was ⁵ .... .
A Oh well!

• Suggestions

2 Choose the correct options.

1 **A** Let's watch that Harry Potter movie tonight.
  B *Good idea! / No way!* I love Rupert Grint.
2 **A** Why *don't / not* we go to the gym?
  B No, thanks. I'm tired.
3 **A** How about *go / going* to the soccer field after school?
  B That's a good idea. We can practice for the game.

• Reasoning

3 Put the conversation in the correct order.

.... Because I don't like museums. They're boring.
.... Why not?
.... No, thanks.
.... Because it's interesting. Do you want to come?
.1.. Why do you want to go to the museum?
.... Oh, OK.

Vocabulary • Sports

1 Complete the sports with the missing letters.

1 *ice hockey*
2 j_d_
3 t_n_ _s
4 b_ _k_tb_ _l
5 b_s_b_ll
6 sn_ _b_ _ _d_ _g
7 _rch_r_
8 h_rs_ba_ _ r_d_ _g

• Compound nouns

2 Match the words on the left (1–7) to the words on the right (a–g).

1 judo   a pool
2 swimming   b belt
3 hockey   c court
4 tennis   d skates
5 football   e field
6 ice   f stick
7 basketball   g racket

• Types of movies

3 Complete the sentences with these words.

animations documentaries ~~horror~~
musical   science fiction   westerns

1 That new *horror* movie was very scary!
2 I don't like watching .... . You learn things, but they're boring.
3 .... are not only about cowboys; they are about life in the American West.
4 The aliens in the .... movie are weird.
5 I enjoyed the songs in the ...., and the story was good, too.
6 .... aren't only for children. Adults enjoy cartoons, too.

• Adjectives

4 Choose the correct options.

1 I don't enjoy football. I think it's *expensive / boring*.
2 Mmm! This popcorn is *weird / tasty*.
3 My best friend is *funny / awesome*. He always tells good jokes.
4 They got married on a beautiful island. It was very *annoying / romantic*.
5 We visited the London Dungeon yesterday. It was *terrible / scary*!
6 That action movie last night was *exciting / tasty*.

• History

5 Complete the sentences with these words.

~~castle~~   century   knight   plague
prisoners   servants   soldiers

1 The king of England built this *castle* in the twelfth .... .
2 There were hundreds of .... in the dungeon.
3 There were thousands of .... in the king's army.
4 The .... had a white horse.
5 The .... washed the clothes and cooked the food.
6 The .... was a terrible disease.

• Life events

6 Match the beginnings (1–6) to the endings (a–f) of the sentences.

1 My baby sister was born c
2 Jay fell
3 Susan went
4 Maria had
5 Rita and Ed moved
6 George found

a a baby when she was thirty.
b a job in New York when he graduated.
c in 2011.
d to a new neighborhood last week.
e in love with a beautiful girl.
f to college in Scotland.

Word list

Unit 1 • Play The Game!

Sports

archery	/ˈɑrtʃəri/
basketball	/ˈbæskɪtˌbɔl/
football	/ˈfʊtbɔl/
gymnastics	/dʒɪmˈnæstɪks/
horseback riding	/ˈhɔrsbæck ˌraɪdɪŋ/
ice hockey	/ˈaɪs ˌhɑki/
ice skating	/ˈaɪs ˌskeɪtɪŋ/
judo	/ˈdʒudoʊ/
mountain biking	/ˈmaʊntˀn ˌbaɪkɪŋ/
skateboarding	/ˈskeɪtbɔrdɪŋ/
skiing	/ˈskiɪŋ/
snowboarding	/ˈsnoʊˌbɔrdɪŋ/
soccer	/ˈsɑkɚ/
swimming	/ˈswɪmɪŋ/
tennis	/ˈtɛnɪs/
track	/træk/

Compound nouns

basketball court	/ˈbæskɪtˌbɔl kɔrt/
football field	/ˈfʊtbɔl fild/
hockey stick	/ˈhɑki ˌstɪk/
ice skates	/ˈaɪs skeɪts/
ice skating rink	/ˈaɪs skeɪtɪŋ ˌrɪŋk/
judo belt	/ˈdʒudoʊ bɛlt/
soccer cleats	/ˈsɑkɚ klits/
soccer field	/ˈsɑkɚ fild/
swimming pool	/ˈswɪmɪŋ pul/
swimsuit	/ˈswɪmsut/
tennis court	/ˈtɛnɪs kɔrt/
tennis racket	/ˈtɛnɪs ˌrækɪt/

Unit 2 • The Big Picture

Types of movies

action movie	/ˈækʃən ˈmuvi/
animation	/ˈænəˌmeɪʃən/
comedy	/ˈkɑmədi/
documentary	/ˌdɑkyəˈmɛntəri/
fantasy	/ˈfæntəsi/
historical movie	/hɪˈstɔrɪkəl ˈmuvi/
horror movie	/ˈhɔrɚ ˈmuvi/
martial arts movie	/ˈmarʃəl arts ˈmuvi/
musical	/ˈmyuzɪkəl/
science fiction movie	/ˌsaɪəns ˈfɪkʃən ˈmuvi/
war movie	/ˈwɔr ˈmuvi/
western	/ˈwɛstɚn/

Adjectives

annoying	/əˈnɔɪ-ɪŋ/
awesome	/ˈɔsəm/
boring	/ˈbɔrɪŋ/
exciting	/ɪkˈsaɪtɪŋ/
expensive	/ɪkˈspɛnsɪv/
funny	/ˈfʌni/
romantic	/roʊˈmæntɪk/
sad	/sæd/
scary	/ˈskɛri/
tasty	/ˈteɪsti/
terrible	/ˈtɛrəbəl/
weird	/wɪrd/

Unit 3 • Past Lives

History

army	/ˈɑrmi/
castle	/ˈkæsəl/
century	/ˈsɛntʃəri/
die	/daɪ/
dungeon	/ˈdʌndʒən/
kill	/kɪl/
king	/kɪŋ/
knight	/naɪt/
plague	/pleɪg/
prisoner	/ˈprɪzənɚ/
queen	/kwin/
servant	/ˈsɚvənt/
soldier	/ˈsoʊldʒɚ/
sword	/sɔrd/
war	/wɔr/

Life events

be born	/bi bɔrn/
die	/daɪ/
fall in love	/fɔl ɪn ˈlʌv/
find a job	/faɪnd ə ˈdʒɑb/
get married	/gɛt ˈmærɪd/
go to college	/goʊ tə ˈkɑlɪdʒ/
graduate	/ˈgrædʒueɪt/
have a baby	/hæv ə ˈbeɪbi/
leave home	/liv ˈhoʊm/
move	/muv/
retire	/rɪˈtaɪɚ/
start school	/start ˈskul/

4 Is It a Crime?

Vocabulary • Breaking the rules

1 Match the pictures to these phrases. Then listen, check and repeat.

2.1

> be rude
> bully
> cheat on an exam
> copy someone's homework
> fight
> lie
> litter
> play loud music
> skip school
> spray graffiti   1
> steal something
> use a cell phone in class

2 Match the phrases in Exercise 1 to the sentences.

1 My friends were at school, but I wasn't.
   skip school
2 Max hit Leo and Leo hit Max.
3 I wrote the answers on my hand.
4 He wrote his name on the classroom wall.
5 She took some CDs, but she didn't pay for them.
6 We can hear our neighbors' stereo at night.
7 They didn't put the paper in the trash can.
8 Lucy didn't do her homework. I gave her mine.
9 She didn't speak nicely to me.
10 I sent her a text message during math class.
11 He took the little boys' money and they cried.
12 She didn't tell the teacher the truth.

3 In pairs, ask and answer questions about breaking rules. Use *always, often, sometimes* or *never*.

Do you litter?

No, I never litter.

**Brain Trainer
Activity 3**
Go to page 61

Reading

1 Look quickly at the text. What type of text do you think it is?

1 A magazine interview
2 A letter in a magazine
3 An email to a magazine

2 Read and check your answer to Exercise 1.

3 Read the text. Are the statements true (T), false (F) or don't know (DK)?

2.2

1 The students were late for school. *F*
2 Oliver was at home.
3 Rob was reading text messages from Oliver.
4 Isabel copied Maria's homework.
5 One of Rob's friends sprayed graffiti.
6 The school rules say students can't use cell phones in class.
7 The principal thought Rob's answer was rude.
8 The principal punished the students in Rob's class.

4 What about you? In pairs, ask and answer.

1 Are you sometimes late for school?
2 Do you or your friends ever skip school?
3 Do you send text messages to your friends during class? Do your friends send you text messages?
4 Are your friends rude to teachers?

> Are you sometimes late for school?

> Yes, I'm often late for school. What about you?

> I'm never late for school.

Paul's Problem Page

★ Letter Of The Week

Hi Paul,

I had a bad day at school yesterday. Let me tell you about it. My friends and I were in the classroom. It was nine twenty and we were waiting for our teacher. She was late. I was alone at my desk because my best friend Oliver was skipping school that day. I was reading some text messages on my cell phone. Two boys from my class, Dan and Marcus, were fighting. Maria was copying Isabel's homework because she never does her own homework. One boy, Carl, was even spraying graffiti on a wall.

Suddenly, Ms. Harris came into the classroom. She was very angry. She stopped in front of my desk, looked at me and said, "Why are you using your cell phone in class? You're breaking the school rules!" "But Ms. Harris, I wasn't using my cell phone. I was only reading some text messages," I said. "Why are you angry with me?" Ms. Harris thought I was lying to her. "Don't be rude, Rob! You are using your cell phone!" she said, and she sent me to the principal's office.

The principal punished me, but he didn't punish anyone else. What can I do?

Rob

Grammar • Past continuous

Affirmative		
I/He/She/It You/We/They	was reading were reading	a text.

Negative		
I/He/She/It You/We/They	wasn't (was not) reading weren't (were not) reading	a text.

Questions and short answers	
Was I/he/she/it reading a text?	Yes, I/he/she/it was. No, I/he/she/it wasn't.
Were you/we/they reading a text?	Yes, you/we/they were. No, you/we/they weren't.

Wh questions	
What were you doing last night?	Why was she cheating?

Time expressions		
yesterday morning	last night	three days ago

Grammar reference page 114

1 **Study the grammar table. Choose the correct option to complete the rule.**

> We use the Past continuous to describe *an action in progress / that finished* at a particular time in the past.

2 **Make sentences with the Past continuous.**

1 at eight o'clock last night / my dad / watch TV
   At eight o'clock last night my dad was watching TV.
2 you / cheat / on the exam!
3 I / sleep / at midnight
4 Julie and Chris / study / at ten o'clock
5 we / send / text messages / in class

3 **Make negative sentences with the Past continuous.**

1 You were lying to your parents.
   You weren't lying to your parents.
2 He was stealing CDs.
3 Our neighbors were playing loud music.
4 She was skipping school.
5 I was spraying graffiti on the walls.

4 **Make questions with the Past continuous.**

1 your friend / wear / jeans / yesterday?
   Was your friend wearing jeans yesterday?
2 your teacher / write / on the board / at the beginning of class?
3 you / watch / TV / at 9 p.m. last night?
4 you and your friends / walk / to school / at 8 a.m. yesterday?
5 what / you / do / yesterday at eleven o'clock?

5 **In pairs, ask and answer the questions in Exercise 4.**

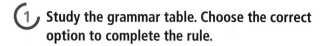

Was your friend wearing jeans yesterday?

Yes, she was.

Pronunciation
was and *were*: strong and weak forms

6a **Listen and repeat the sentences.**
2.3
1 Was he listening to music? (weak)
2 Yes, he was. (strong)
3 Were they cheating on the exam? (weak)
4 No, they weren't. (strong)
5 They weren't cheating. (strong)

b **Read the sentences. Is *was/were* strong (S) or weak (W)?**

1 Were they playing football? W
2 Yes, they were.
3 They weren't doing yoga.
4 He was watching TV.
5 Was she waiting for us?

c **Listen, check and repeat.**
2.4

7 **What about you? What were you doing at 8 p.m. last night? Write sentences.**

Vocabulary • Prepositions of movement

1 Match the pictures to these prepositions of movement. Then listen, check and repeat.

2.5

across	along	around	down	into	off
out of	over	through	under	up	1

Word list page 57
Workbook page 119

Brain Trainer
Activity 4
Go to page 61

2 Complete the sentences with a preposition of movement. Then listen and check.

2.6

1 At 8:30 p.m. Bill Smith was walking *under* a bridge.
2 At 8:35 p.m. he was running .... a road.
3 At 8:50 p.m. he was walking .... a hotel.
4 At 9:00 p.m. he was walking .... a room.
5 At 9:14 p.m. he was taking money .... a bag.
6 At 9:15 p.m. he was climbing .... a window.
7 At 9:20 p.m. he was climbing .... a ladder.
8 At 9:25 p.m. he was jumping .... a wall.
9 At 9:30 p.m. he was riding a motorcycle .... a hill.
10 At 9:35 p.m. he was walking .... a wall.
11 At 9:37 p.m. he was falling .... a wall.

Speaking and Listening

1 Look at the photo. Answer the questions.

1 Where are the friends?
2 What do you think Jody is saying to Nadia?

2 Listen and read the conversation.
2.7 Check your answers.

3 Listen and read again. Answer the questions.
2.7
1 Which two things did Nadia lose?
   Nadia lost her cell phone and her purse.
2 How does she think she lost them?
3 Did she take the bus to the bowling alley?
4 Who calls Jody?
5 Where is Nadia's cell phone?
6 How does Nadia feel in the end?

4 Act out the conversation in groups of four.

Jody	Nadia! Finally! Where were you? Zak was calling you.
Nadia	You'll never guess! A thief took my cell phone—and my purse!
Zak	Really? What happened?
Nadia	Well, I was waiting at the bus stop when a man bumped into me. When the bus arrived, I didn't have my purse or my cell phone.
Zak	Oh no! What did you do?
Nadia	I walked to the bowling alley.
Zak	Poor thing!
Zak	Is that your cell phone, Jody?
Jody	It is. Hello?
Nadia's mom	Hello, Jody. It's Nadia's mom. Please tell her she left her cell phone and purse at home.
Jody	Of course. Bye. Nadia, that guy at the bus stop wasn't a thief. You left your cell phone and purse at home.
Nadia	Really? That's great!

Say it in your language ...
Finally!
You'll never guess!

5 Look back at the conversation. Who says what?

1 You'll never guess! *Nadia*
2 What happened?
3 Oh no!
4 What did you do?
5 Poor thing!
6 Really? That's great!

6 Read the phrases for showing interest.

Good news	Neutral	Bad news
That's great! That's amazing!	Really?	Oh no! Poor thing!

7 Listen to the conversation. Act out the conversation in pairs.

2.8

Zak Hi, Nadia. What were you doing ¹ at 4:00 p.m.? I was waiting for you.

Nadia I was ² leaving my house when I saw ³ Shakira. ⁴ She was walking across the street.

Zak Really? What did you do?

Nadia I ⁵ took a photo of her.

Zak That's amazing!

8 Work in pairs. Replace the words in purple in Exercise 7. Use these words and/or your own ideas. Act out the conversation.

> What were you doing yesterday evening? I was waiting for you.

> I was sitting in a café.

1 yesterday afternoon / yesterday evening / at three o'clock

2 sitting in a café / walking in the park / getting off the bus

3 Justin Bieber / Mark and Sue / a lost child

4 talking on the phone / waiting for a taxi / stealing a woman's purse / asking for help

5 said hello / invited them to my party / took him/her to the police station

Grammar • Past simple and Past continuous

when	*while*
I was waiting at the bus stop when a thief stole my bag.	While I was waiting at the bus stop, a thief stole my bag.

Grammar reference page 114

1 Study the grammar table. Choose the correct options to complete the rule.

> We use *while* / *when* with the Past continuous and *while* / *when* with the Past simple.

2 Choose the correct options.

1 While I *waited* / *was waiting* for the bus, I *saw* / *was seeing* my friend.
2 While we *copied* / *were copying* the answers, the teacher *saw* / *was seeing* us.
3 They *had* / *were having* dinner when the phone *rang* / *was ringing*.
4 What *did you do* / *were you doing* when they *arrived* / *were arriving*?
5 Maria *came* / *was coming* to the front door while she *ate* / *was eating a snack*.

3 Complete the sentences with the Past simple or the Past continuous.

1 While we *were swimming* (swim), we *saw* (see) some dolphins in the water.
2 The students .... (have) class when they .... (hear) a noise outside.
3 My sister .... (fall) out of bed while she .... (sleep).
4 Mark .... (sit) in the yard when a neighbor .... (come) to visit.
5 Who .... (you / see) while you .... (stay) at the beach?

4 What about you? Write four sentences with *when* and *while* in your notebook.

I was watching TV when the phone rang.

Reading

1 **Look quickly at the text. What type of text is it?**

1 A movie review
2 A newspaper article
3 A magazine interview

Mrs. Emily Hill, 71: Supergranny!

Supergranny Catches Thieves!

Two young thieves got the scare of their lives when they tried to steal a woman's bag yesterday morning.

Mrs. Emily Hill (71) of Boston was sitting in the Public Garden with a friend, Mrs. Rosie Williams (69). "We were enjoying the sunshine and talking," said Mrs. Hill. "There weren't many people in the park because it was early in the morning. Two boys were looking at the ducks. They were only about fifteen, but they weren't in school. I guess they were skipping school. One of the boys came up to us and asked us the time. I was looking at my watch when the other boy grabbed my bag. Both boys ran away."

Mrs. Hill was shocked, but she jumped up and ran after them. "I didn't want to lose my money, my cell phone or the photos of my grandchildren," she said.

The boys ran across the park and into a hotel. Mrs. Hill followed them. A young waiter, Bruno Rossi (23), caught one of the boys. The other boy was not so lucky. He was trying to escape when Mrs. Hill stopped him with a judo throw. "I have a black belt in judo," Mrs. Hill told our reporter. "And I also go jogging every day. I was a star athlete when I was young."

Who needs Superman when you're a Supergranny?

Key Words

scare	guess
came up to us	grabbed
a judo throw	reporter

2 **Read and check your answer to Exercise 1.**

3 **Read the text again. Are the statements true (T)**
2.9 **or false (F)?**

1 It was early in the morning. *T*
2 There were many people in the park.
3 The thieves tried to steal a watch.
4 The boys ran into a hotel.
5 Mrs. Hill has a brown belt in judo.

4 **Read the text again. Answer the questions.**
2.9
1 How old is Mrs. Hill? *She's 71.*
2 What were the boys doing when Mrs. Hill first saw them?
3 How did Mrs. Hill feel when the boys stole her bag?
4 What was in Mrs. Hill's bag?
5 Who caught the boys?
6 What sports does Mrs. Hill do?

Listening

1 **Listen to the police interviews with three people.**
2.10 **Match each person (A–C) to the interview (1–3).**

A Mr. White, the Parkview Hotel manager
B Robert Green, a teenager
C Bruno Rossi, a waiter at the hotel restaurant

2 **Listen again. Choose the correct answer.**
2.10
1 Who took the bag?
a the waiter   b Rob   c Sam
2 Who stopped the first boy?
a Mrs. Hill   b the waiter   c the manager
3 What did the manager do?
a He called the police.
b He shouted at the boys.
c He sat on one of the thieves.

Writing • A short story

1 Read the Writing File.

> **Writing File** Sequencing words
>
> We use sequencing words to show the order of events. We use them at the beginning of sentences.
>
> - **First, …**
> - **Then … / Next, …**
> - **Finally, …**

2 Read the short story about Ed Badman. Find the sequencing words.

The Unlucky Thief

It was midnight and it was raining when Ed Badman arrived at the DVD store. First, Ed climbed up the wall. Next, he broke a window, went through it and jumped down into the store. He stole DVDs, MP3 players and a DVD player. Then he tried to leave through the back door, but it was locked.

Ed had an idea. He climbed onto an old chair and tried to climb through the broken window. Unfortunately, the chair broke. Ed fell off the chair and broke his leg. Finally, the police arrived. "I want to go home!" Ed told them. The police took him away in the police car—not home, but to jail!

3 Choose the correct options.

¹ *First, / Finally,* I got up. ² *Then / First,* I had breakfast. ³ *Next, / Finally,* I walked to school and went to my classes. ⁴ *Finally, / First,* I came home and did my homework.

4 Read the story about Ed Badman again. Answer the questions.

1 What time was it when Ed arrived at the store?
  It was midnight when Ed arrived at the store.
2 What was the weather like?
3 How did he get into the store?
4 What did he try to steal?
5 Why didn't he leave through the back door?
6 Why did Ed climb onto a chair?
7 What happened to Ed?

5 Think of your own short story. Answer the questions. Take notes.

1 What time was it?
2 What was the weather like?
3 Who was there?
4 What did they do?
5 Why did they do it?
6 What happened?

6 Write a short story. Use "My short story" and your notes from Exercise 5.

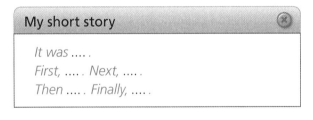

> **My short story**
>
> *It was ….. .*
> *First, ….. . Next, ….. .*
> *Then ….. . Finally, ….. .*

> **Remember!**
> - Use sequencing words.
> - Use the vocabulary in this unit.
> - Check your grammar, spelling and punctuation.

Refresh Your Memory!

Grammar • Review

1 **Make sentences and questions with the correct form of the Past continuous.**

1 Luke and Jessica / play / basketball / at ten o'clock
   Luke and Jessica were playing basketball at ten o'clock.
2 Monica / not watch / TV / at midnight last night
3 you / ride / your bike / in the park / yesterday afternoon?
4 I / listen to / my MP3 player / at five o'clock
5 we / not work / in the store / yesterday morning
6 Lily / do / her homework?
7 I / not eat / a sandwich

2 **Complete the sentences with the correct form of the Past simple or Past continuous.**

1 She *was standing* (stand) on a chair when she *fell* (fall) and *broke* (break) her leg.
2 When the phone .... (ring), Jason .... (read) a book.
3 Sally and Mike .... (copy) Jane's homework when the teacher .... (come) into the room.
4 While we .... (wait) for the bus, a thief .... (steal) my bag.
5 I .... (meet) them while they .... (walk) home from school.
6 While you .... (sleep), the cat .... (eat) your dinner.
7 The boys .... (spray) graffiti while Mr. James .... (write) on the board.

3 **Complete the sentences with *when* or *while*.**

1 I was studying for a test *when* Alan arrived.
2 .... she was walking in the park, she saw Lucy.
3 Dad was sleeping on the sofa .... Mom came home.
4 It started to rain .... we were waiting for the bus.
5 .... we arrived at the party, people were dancing.
6 .... we were talking, the waiter brought our meal.
7 Lucy was using her phone in class .... the teacher asked her a question.

Vocabulary • Review

4 **Complete the sentences with these words.**

| ~~copy~~ litter fight lie spray were |

1 I never *copy* my friend's homework.
2 Do you .... with your sister?
3 They didn't .... to their parents. They told the truth.
4 .... you rude to the teacher?
5 I sometimes .... in the street.
6 My sister didn't .... graffiti on the walls.

5 **Look at the pictures. Complete the sentences with these words.**

| across around into ~~over~~ under up |

1 The dog is jumping *over* a box.
2 It's running .... a bridge.
3 It's climbing .... a tree.
4 It's climbing .... a car.
5 It's running .... the man.
6 It's running .... the street.

Speaking • Review

6
2.11 **Complete the conversation with these words. Then listen and check.**

| do really ~~what~~ when |

James [1] *What* were you doing at 3 p.m.?
Lisa I was in the store. I was looking at some books [2] .... I saw a girl take a magazine.
James Then what did she [3] .... ?
Lisa She put the magazine in her bag.
James [4] .... ?

Dictation

7
2.12 **Listen and write in your notebook.**

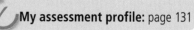
My assessment profile: page 131

Angelica Da Silva's Profile

👤 **Age**

14 years old

Home country	City
US	Philadelphia

My favorite …

music	hip hop
artists	Picasso; Jane Golden (from the Mural Arts Program)
things	art and music!

Reading

1 Read Angelica's profile. Are the statements true (T) or false (F)?

1 Angelica lives in New York. *F*
2 Angelica likes hip hop.
3 Angelica's favorite things are movies and art.

2 Read the article. Answer the questions.

2.13

1 What does Angelica do on the weekends?
   She becomes an artist.
2 When was graffiti a big problem in Philadelphia?
3 What did the people of Philadelphia do about it?
4 What is a mural?
5 Who joined the Mural Arts Program?
6 When did Angelica join the program?
7 Who does Angelica help?

Angelica's Mural

Angelica Da Silva is 14 years old. She lives in Philadelphia, in the US. From Monday to Friday Angelica goes to school, but every weekend she becomes an artist! She works with the Philadelphia Mural Arts Program.

Thirty years ago, horrible graffiti covered many buildings in Philadelphia. The people of the city weren't happy about this, but what could they do? In the end, they found an answer to the problem. They started the Mural Arts Program. Murals are beautiful, big paintings on the walls of buildings. Many teenagers from Philadelphia joined the Mural Arts Program. These young people often had problems at home and school. The Mural Arts Program helped these teenagers. Through the program, they learned about art and became artists.

Angelica joined the Mural Arts Program in 2011. Now she paints beautiful pictures on the walls of many city buildings. First, she chooses a wall. Then she asks the owner's permission to paint it. Next, she designs a mural with the help of the teachers in the program. Finally, she paints the wall with her friends. It's really exciting!

Angelica paints every weekend. She also teaches young children to paint. The Mural Arts Program helped her a lot, and now she's helping other teenagers.

Class discussion

1 What big cities are there in your country?
2 Is graffiti a problem where you live?
3 Do you like the mural in the photo?
4 Would you like a mural in your school or street?

Grammar • Past continuous

1 **Complete the sentences with the correct form of the Past continuous.**

1 At nine o'clock yesterday morning I *was talking* (talk) to my science teacher.
2 At three o'clock Sam and Lisa .... (play) soccer.
3 At two thirty we .... (walk) home from school.
4 At five o'clock you .... (study) in the library.
5 At nine o'clock on Saturday Marco .... (sleep).

2 **Make sentences with the Past continuous.**

1 Matthew / listen / to music / last night ✓
  – he / watch / TV ✗
  Matthew was listening to music last night.
  He wasn't watching TV.
2 we / have / dinner / at eight ✗ – we / have / breakfast ✓
3 my parents / drive / home / from work / last night ✗
  – they / cook / a meal ✓
4 I / study / for my exam / yesterday ✓
  – I / write / my blog ✗
5 Della and Nancy / go / store / on Saturday ✗
  – they / visit / their grandparents ✓

3 **Make questions and answers.**

1 Sonya / do / homework? ✓
  Was Sonya doing her homework? Yes, she was.
2 Anya and Adam / fight? ✓
3 Barbara / copy / her friend's homework? ✗
4 Danny and Freddie / play / loud music? ✗
5 Ian / do / an exercise? ✓

• Past simple and Past continuous

4 **Complete the text with the Past simple or Past continuous.**

Last night I ¹ *was studying* (study) for my exam when my little brother ² .... (come) into my room. He ³ .... (want) to use my laptop, but I ⁴ .... (use) it. While we ⁵ .... (fight), my mom ⁶ .... (come) into my room. She ⁷ .... (tell) us to stop fighting, but we ⁸ .... (shout) and we ⁹ .... (not hear) her. She wasn't happy!

5 **Complete the sentences with *when* or *while*.**

1 We were waiting for the bus *when* we saw Jody.
2 The thief was stealing some DVDs .... the police officer saw him.
3 .... they were listening to the teacher, Amanda's cell phone rang.
4 My mom heard a noise in the yard .... she was watching TV.
5 The cat was climbing the tree .... it fell down.
6 They arrived .... we were having dinner.

• Comparatives

6 **Complete the sentences with the comparatives.**

1 The math exam was *easier* (easy) than the history exam.
2 The movie was interesting, but the book was .... (interesting).
3 My grades are bad, but your grades are .... (bad).
4 Ben is .... (thin) than his brother.
5 My hair is .... (curly) than Lisa's.
6 Skiing is .... (dangerous) than swimming.

• Superlatives

7 **Complete the sentences with the superlatives.**

1 The Antarctic is *the coldest* (cold) place in the world.
2 What is .... (dangerous) animal in Australia?
3 The .... (long) river in the world is the Nile River.
4 I have .... (good) friends in the world!
5 Laura is .... (funny) person in my class.
6 Uncle Jim is .... (generous) person in the world!

• Present continuous for future

8 **Complete the phone conversation with the Present continuous.**

Max Hi, Eva. What ¹ *are you doing* (you / do) tomorrow afternoon?
Eva Hi, Max. Well, I ² .... (not study) for my exams. I ³ .... (go) to the movies with Joel.
Max ⁴ .... (Susanna / come) with you?
Eva No, she isn't. She ⁵ .... (play) in a basketball game.
Max Oh, never mind. Can I come with you?
Eva Sure. We ⁶ .... (meet) outside the movie theater at 2 p.m. See you then!

• Going to

9 **Make sentences with *going to*.**

1 It's Mom's birthday tomorrow and we*'re going to buy* (buy) her a present.
2 I .... (not throw) those magazines away.
  I .... (recycle) them.
3 What .... (you / do) when you finish school?
4 The children .... (clean) the beach up.
5 Dave .... (not play) his computer game.
  He .... (watch) a DVD.
6 What color .... (they / paint) the kitchen?

• Should/Shouldn't

10 **Complete the conversations with *should* or *shouldn't*.**

1 **A** I don't feel well.
  B You *should* go to the doctor.
2 **A** I can't play that song on my guitar.
  B You .... practice more.
3 **A** I'm going to put the glass jar in the trash can.
  B You .... do that. Why don't you recycle it?
4 **A** I'm very tired.
  B You .... go to bed earlier.
5 **A** It's midnight. I'm going home now.
  B You .... walk home alone; it's dangerous.
6 **A** I have a lot of old clothes.
  B You .... throw them away. You .... recycle them.

• Must/Mustn't

11 **Choose the correct option.**

1 Shh! You *must / mustn't* talk in the library.
2 The students *must / mustn't* study tonight. They have a test tomorrow.
3 Our plane leaves at nine. We *must / mustn't* be at the airport at seven.
4 You *must / mustn't* play loud music in your room.
5 We *must / mustn't* protect the planet.
6 You *must / mustn't* use your cell phone in class.

Speaking • Showing interest

1 **Put the conversation in the correct order.**

.... I hurt my leg while I was running.
.1. What's wrong?
.... Really? That was a dangerous thing to do!
.... Oh no! Poor thing! What happened?
.... Yes. I know.
.... A thief tried to steal my cell phone, but I ran after him and stopped him.

• Agreeing and disagreeing

2 **Complete the conversations with these words.**

| agree | don't think | maybe | right | ~~think~~ |

1 **A** I ¹ *think* this is the nicest bag in the store.
  B Yes, I ² .... , but it's also the most expensive.
2 **A** Do you think my dad looks like Bruce Willis?
  B Hmm, ³ .... . He doesn't have any hair.
  A They have the same face.
  B You're ⁴ .... , but Bruce Willis is older than your dad!
3 **A** Who's that boy?
  B That's Jake. He's new in our class.
  A Wow! He's really handsome.
  B I ⁵ .... so. I think Sam's cuter.

• Shopping

3 **Put the conversation in the correct order.**

.... Great. How much is it?
.1. Can I help you?
.... Oh, that's expensive! I don't want it, thanks.
.... Yes, please. Do you have a soccer shirt?
.... It's $85.
.... Yes, we do. Here you go.

Vocabulary • Breaking the rules

1 **Choose the correct options.**

1 Look! Those boys *are stealing / spraying* magazines from the store.
2 Were you *cheating / copying* your friend's homework?
3 Why is he *spraying / playing* graffiti on that wall?
4 What were you *fighting / stealing* with your brother about?
5 Did you *lie / play* to your parents about the party?
6 You mustn't *leave / bully* trash in the street.

• Prepositions of movement

2 **Complete the sentences with these words.**

into	off	out of	over	up	under

1 The thief walked *into* the bank.
2 The cat climbed .... the tree.
3 We took the present .... the box.
4 The boat went .... the bridge.
5 Mark jumped .... the wall.
6 The bridge is .... the river.

• Appearance adjectives

3 **Complete the descriptions with these words.**

beard	big		brown	curly	glasses
green	mustache		straight	~~thin~~	

Gerry is short and ¹ *thin*. He has ² .... black hair. He has a ³ .... and he wears ⁴ .... . His eyes are ⁵ .... . Gerry's best friend, Kevin, is tall and ⁶ .... . He has ⁷ .... brown hair. He has a ⁸ .... . His eyes are ⁹ .... .

• Personality adjectives

4 **Match the adjectives (1–6) to the sentences (a–f).**

1 unfriendly f
2 lazy
3 cheerful
4 friendly
5 moody
6 generous

a She's usually happy and she smiles a lot.
b He likes giving things to other people.
c She likes people and she is nice to them.
d He changes all the time. One minute he's happy and the next minute he's sad.
e She hates working and studying.
f He isn't nice to people and he doesn't help them.

• The environment

5 **Complete the sentences with these words.**

cleaned ... up	planted	~~polluted~~
saved	threw ... away	turned ... off

1 The fish in the river died because people *polluted* the water.
2 Dad .... flowers and vegetables in the garden last spring.
3 The man didn't die because the doctor .... him.
4 I'm sad because Mom .... my old toys .... .
5 She .... the lights .... when she left the room.
6 They made dinner, and then they .... the kitchen .... .

• Materials and containers

6 **Make containers with one word from A and one word from B.**

A cardboard	glass (x2)	metal	paper	plastic
B bag (x2)	bottle	box	can	jar

1 *glass jar*

Word list

Unit 4 • Is It a Crime?

Breaking the rules

be rude	/bi ˈrud/
bully	/ˈbʊli/
cheat on an exam	/ˌtʃit ɔn ən ɪgˈzæm/
copy someone's homework	/ˈkɑpi sʌmwʌnz ˈhoʊmwək/
fight	/faɪt/
lie	/laɪ/
litter	/ˈlɪt̬ ə/
play loud music	/ˌpleɪ laʊd ˈmyuzɪk/
skip school	/ˌskɪp ˈskul/
spray graffiti	/ˌspreɪ grəˈfit̬i/
steal something	/stil ˈsʌmθɪŋ/
use a cell phone in class	/yuz ə ˈsɛl foʊn ɪn ˈklæs/

Prepositions of movement

across	/əˈkrɔs/
along	/əˈlɔŋ/
around	/əˈraʊnd/
down	/daʊn/
into	/ˈɪntə/
off	/ɔf/
out of	/aʊt əv/
over	/ˈoʊvə/
through	/θru/
under	/ˈʌndə/
up	/ʌp/

Unit 5 • Look at You

Appearance adjectives and nouns

beard	/bɪrd/
big	/bɪg/
black	/blæk/
blond	/blɑnd/
blue	/blu/
brown	/braʊn/
curly	/ˈkəli/
dark	/dɑrk/
glasses	/ˈglæsɪz/
gray	/greɪ/
green	/grin/
long	/lɔŋ/
mustache	/ˈmʌstæʃ/
red	/rɛd/
short	/ʃɔrt/
straight	/streɪt/
tall	/tɔl/
thin	/θɪn/

Personality adjectives

cheerful	/ˈtʃɪrfəl/
friendly	/ˈfrɛndli/
generous	/ˈdʒɛnərəs/
hardworking	/hardˈwəkɪŋ/
lazy	/ˈleɪzi/
moody	/ˈmudi/
selfish	/ˈsɛlfɪʃ/
shy	/ʃaɪ/
smart	/smɑrt/
stupid	/ˈstupɪd/
talkative	/ˈtɔkət̬ ɪv/
unfriendly	/ʌnˈfrɛndli/

Unit 6 • It's Your World

Environment verbs

clean up	/ˌklin ˈʌp/
cut down	/ˌkʌt ˈdaʊn/
damage	/ˈdæmɪdʒ/
plant	/plænt/
pollute	/pəˈlut/
protect	/prəˈtɛkt/
recycle	/riˈsaɪkəl/
reuse	/riˈyuz/
save	/seɪv/
throw away	/ˌθroʊ əˈweɪ/
turn off	/ˌtən ˈɔf/
waste	/weɪst/

Materials and containers

bag	/bæg/
bottle	/ˈbɑt̬ l/
box	/bɑks/
can	/kæn/
cardboard	/ˈkɑrdbɔrd/
carton	/ˈkɑrtˀn/
glass	/glæs/
jar	/dʒɑr/
metal	/ˈmɛt̬ l/
paper	/ˈpeɪpə/
plastic	/ˈplæstɪk/
wooden	/ˈwʊdn/

Brain Trainer

Find the difference ⟳

1. Look at the photo on page 14 for one minute. Now study this photo. What differences can you find?

Grammar ⟳

2. Make questions with words from the orange, purple and blue boxes and *do/does*. You have three minutes!

Does our teacher play basketball?

| your mom | your dad | our teacher | your friends |

| do | play | go | watch | call | have |

archery	basketball
judo	homework
mountain biking	skateboarding
sports on television	swimming

Vocabulary ⟳

3. Look at the letters. Guess the sport.

1. *ati* ice skating
2. *ors*
3. *che*
4. *ske*
5. *mna*
6. *oun*

4a. Read the items in the box aloud three times. Cover the box. Read the list below aloud. Which item is missing?

> tennis racket
> basketball court
> ice skates   soccer cleats
> hockey stick   football field

soccer cleats   football field   hockey stick
basketball court   ice skates

4b. Now try again.

> tennis court   ice skating rink
> judo belt   soccer field
> swimming pool   swimsuit

ice skating rink   swimsuit
soccer field   swimming pool   tennis court

Brain Trainer ②

Find the difference

1 Look at the photo on page 24 for one minute. Now study this photo. What differences can you find?

Grammar

2 Unscramble the words. Then match the sentences to the photos.

1 I'm aghtwnic a rohror movie.
I'm watching a horror movie. c
2 They're gnatiwi outside the umemsu.
3 He's ardnige a zagnimae at the moment.
4 We're kinmga a tairalm rats movie.
5 Suzy's digno her ngEilhs homework now.
6 She's tnagki photos at the krpa today.

Vocabulary

3 Follow the letters to find seven types of movies. You can go up, down or diagonally—from the left or from the right.

START	U	S	I	C	A	B	Y	K	P
A	M	Y	N	C	L	F	E	H	D
C	E	D	M	S	E	A	N	T	N
O	M	F	O	T	L	G	W	A	O
B	E	J	V	R	S	D	P	S	Y
D	T	K	I	A	L	O	P	Y	M
C	H	D	E	L	A	W	E	A	B
Z	K	O	Q	A	I	T	R	E	N
X	O	C	C	A	S	H	H	E	L
U	W	U	T	R	S	T	V	U	J
J	Q	M	I	D	G	Y	W	E	S
K	P	E	N	T	A	R	A	Q	T
L	R	O	R	R	O	H	N	R	E

4 Make words. Each word has three shapes.

an-noy-ing

Brain Trainer

Find the difference

1. Look at the photo on page 34 for one minute. Now study this photo. What differences can you find?

Grammar

2. Make sentences with words of the same color. Then make your own color puzzle. In pairs, complete your partner's puzzle.

   You started school seven years ago.

You	We	were	seven	years
night	ago	moved	born	You
years	study	started	ago	fourteen
last	I	watched	school	last
You	TV	yesterday	didn't	year
year	night	leave	her	moved
did	We	a	They	last
didn't	He	last	big	the
homework	city	mistake	She	made

Vocabulary

3. In pairs, look at the pictures. Say one history word about the picture. Your partner says another history word about the picture.

4. Match the timeline of Janet's life (1–6) to the pictures (a–f). Then complete the sentences.

   1 1947: *a* Janet started *school.*
   2 1960: .... Janet went ....
   3 1963: .... Janet...
   4 1974: .... Janet got ....
   5 1978: .... Janet ....
   6 2012: .... Janet ....

Brain Trainer

Find the difference

1 Look at the photo on page 48 for one minute. Now study this photo. What differences can you find?

Grammar

2 Look at the picture for two minutes, then cover it. Now say a square. Your partner says what the person was doing.

> 1d

> The men were fighting.

Vocabulary

3 Read the phrases for two minutes. Cover the list and write the phrases in your notebook. How many can you remember?

spray graffiti	bully
be rude	fight
lie	steal something
litter	use a cell phone in class
cheat on an exam	copy someone's homework
play loud music	skip school

4 Complete the sentences with the correct preposition of movement.

a The dog ran ¹ *around* the tree.
b She climbed ².... the ladder.
c They didn't walk ³.... the bridge. They walked ⁴.... the bridge.
d The cat jumped ⁵.... the wall.
e Lucy was taking the present ⁶.... the box when her mom walked ⁷.... the room.
f Dad was climbing ⁸.... the ladder when the cat ran ⁹.... the road.

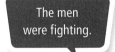

a   b   c   d

Reading

1 Read about the main English-speaking countries.
3.39 **Which country has the biggest population?**

2 Read about the main English-speaking countries
3.39 **again. Answer the questions.**

1 Which famous people came from Dublin?
2 Which place in America sees the sun rise first?
3 What is the capital of Australia?
4 Which country has three capital cities?
5 What was special about the 2010 World Cup?

Your culture

3 **In pairs, answer the questions.**

1 What is the capital of your country?
2 What is the population and currency?
3 What is interesting about your country?

4 **Write a short fact file about your country. Use your answers to Exercise 3 and the English-speaking countries examples to help you.**

Canada
Capital of Canada: Ottawa
Population of Canada: about 34,019,000
Currency: Canadian dollar
Extra interesting facts: They speak French and English in Canada.

Australia
Capital of Australia: Canberra
Population of Australia: about 22,600,000
Currency: Australian dollar
Extra interesting facts: There are more sheep in Australia than people!

India
Capital of India: New Delhi
Population of India: 1.2 billion
Currency: Indian rupee
Extra interesting facts: India makes between 800 and 1,000 Bollywood movies every year.

New Zealand
Capital of New Zealand: Wellington
Population of New Zealand: about 4,300,000
Currency: New Zealand dollar
Extra interesting facts: It is the first country in the world to see the sun rise!

South Africa
Capitals of South Africa: Pretoria, Cape Town and Bloemfontein
Population of South Africa: 49,991,300
Currency: South African rand
Extra interesting facts: The Soccer World Cup took place in South Africa in 2010. This was the first Soccer World Cup in Africa.

The UK
Capital of the UK and England: London (Edinburgh is the capital of Scotland. Belfast is the capital of Northern Ireland. Cardiff is the capital of Wales.)
Population of the UK: about 63 million
Full name: United Kingdom of Great Britain and Northern Ireland
Currency: British pound
Extra interesting facts: The English like drinking tea! An English person drinks more tea than anyone else. They drink over twenty times more than Americans.

The Republic of Ireland
Capital of the Republic of Ireland: Dublin
Population of the Republic of Ireland: 4,470,700
Currency: The euro
Extra interesting facts: In the Republic of Ireland, people also speak Gaelic. English is the language of business. Ireland is famous for its writers. James Joyce and Oscar Wilde came from Dublin.

The US
Capital of the US: Washington, DC
Population of the US: 310,000,000
Full name: United States of America
Currency: US dollar
Extra interesting facts: The state of Maine sees the sun rise before the other states!

Reading

1 Read about the US. How many states are there
3.40 **in the US?**

2 Read about the US again. Answer the questions.
3.40
1 Is the US a multicultural country? Why?
2 What is the capital of the US? Why is this city important?
3 What's the "Big Apple"?
4 Which famous buildings are in New York?
5 What's the weather like in LA?

3 In pairs, answer the questions.
1 What is the largest city in your country?
2 What is your favorite city in your country?
3 What other cities do you know in Europe and the US?

4 Write a short paragraph about your favorite city in your country. Use your answers to Exercise 3 and the US examples to help you.

The US

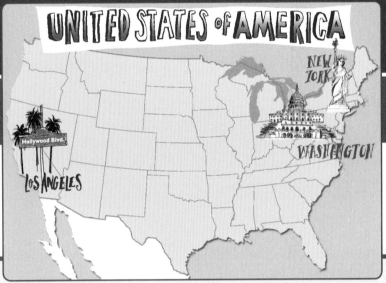

The US has 50 states, and they are all different.
In the US, there is great variety in climate, landscape, cities and culture.
People from all over the world live there.
The US is very multicultural.

DC

Washington, DC, is the capital of the US. It is a very important city. The president and his family live in Washington, DC, in the White House. The White House has tennis courts, a swimming pool and a movie theater for the president's family. Inside the White House is the Oval Office. It is the office of the president. Many leaders from around the world travel to the Oval Office to meet the President.

I love NYC
The "Big Apple" has a population of 8.2 million people. The New York
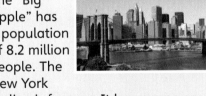
skyline is famous. It has some very tall buildings called skyscrapers. The Empire State Building and the Chrysler Building are easy to recognize. The Statue of Liberty is in New York Harbor. It was a present from the people of France to the US. It is a symbol of freedom and democracy.

City of Angels
Los Angeles (LA) is very multicultural. People from all over the world live, work and

enjoy the good weather in LA. The city has many important centers of culture, science and technology, and it is the movie capital of the world! You can see the famous Hollywood sign in the hills of the city. You can also walk down Hollywood Boulevard and see the handprints of famous actors.

Culture ③ Australia – Nature

Reading

1 Read about Australia. **Is Australia a continent, a country or an island?**
3.41

2 Read about Australia again.
3.41 **Answer the questions.**

1 Do children go to school in the Outback?
2 What is the official name for "Ayers Rock"?
3 How many beaches are there in Australia?
4 What can you see from space?
5 What are the "Three Sisters"?

Your culture

3 **In pairs, answer the questions.**

1 What country and continent do you live in?
2 What is special about nature in your country?
3 Do you know an old story about your country? Tell your partner.

4 Write a short paragraph about nature in your country. Use your answers to Exercise 3 and the Australia examples to help you.

AUSTRALIA

Australia is a continent, a country and an island. It is very famous for its nature. It has 550 national parks and 15 World Heritage Sites. In Australia you can see mountains, salt lakes, deserts, rain forests, coral reefs and amazing beaches!

The Outback

The Outback is a part of Australia where few people live. It is often dry like a desert. Many families work on big sheep farms and live hundreds of kilometers away from towns or schools. Children in these families don't go to school. They learn at home and speak to their teachers over the Internet! A famous natural beauty in the Outback is "Ayers Rock." Its official name is *Uluru*. Almost half a million people visit *Uluru* every year.

The coast

There are over 10,000 beaches in Australia! The Great Barrier Reef is on the northeast coast of Australia. It is a marine park over 3,000 kilometers long! It is longer than the Great Wall of China, and you can see it from space. It is famous for its natural beauty. The reef has many colorful corals and is home to whales, dolphins, turtles and crocodiles!

Mountains

The Blue Mountains are in the southeast of Australia. In the Blue Mountains, there are three famous rocks called the "Three Sisters." The Aborigine people have a very old story about the rocks. The story is about three beautiful women. The women fall in love with three brothers. The brothers are from a different tribe, so they can't get married. The brothers try to catch the sisters. To protect the sisters, a magician changes them into rocks!

MOVE IT!

WORKBOOK WITH MP3S

SPLIT EDITION

2A

SUZANNE GAYNOR

SERIES CONSULTANT: CARA NORRIS-RAMIREZ

Contents

Starter Unit

Grammar • To be

1 **Choose the correct options.**

1 My best friend *is* Spanish.
   a am   (b) is   c are
2 The pens .... on the table in my room.
   a am not   b isn't   c aren't
3 I .... in an English class.
   a am   b is   c are
4 James .... happy today.
   a are   b aren't   c isn't
5 .... you in the backyard?
   a Am   b Is   c Are
6 We .... in the living room.
   a aren't   b isn't   c is

2 **Complete the conversation.**

Max	Hi! ¹ *My name's* (my name / be) Max. ² .... (you / be) Emily?
Emily	Yes, ³ .... (I / be). Hi, Max.
Max	⁴ .... (you / be) German?
Emily	No, ⁵ .... (I / be).
Max	⁶ .... (this / be) your book?
Emily	No, ⁷ .... (it / be).
Max	⁸ .... (these / be) your pens?
Emily	No, ⁹ .... (they / be).

• Have

3 **Write sentences and questions with the correct form of *have*.**

1 Jack / a new MP3 player. ✓
   Jack has a new MP3 player.
2 you / a present / for your mother's birthday **?**
   ....
3 she / a black cat ✗
   ....
4 we / a good computer game ✓
   ....
5 they / a big backyard ✗
   ....
6 your cousins / a house near the beach **?**
   ....

4 **Complete the text with the correct form of *is* or *has*.**

Max ¹ *is* a student, but he ² .... at school today. He ³ .... at home in the living room. He ⁴ .... ten math exercises for homework, but his math book ⁵ .... in his backpack next to him. Max's dog, Bubbles, ⁶ .... in the living room, too. Bubbles ⁷ .... a big dog. She ⁸ .... a very small dog, and she ⁹ .... very short legs. Can you see her? She ¹⁰ .... under the chair.

• There is/are

5 Write questions and answers with the correct form of *there is/are*.

1 an apple on the table? ✘ (an egg)
  A *Is there an apple on the table?*
  B *No, there isn't. There's an egg on the table.*
2 two cats in the house? ✔ (two big cats)
  A ....
  B ....
3 a bike in the yard? ✔ (a red bike)
  A ....
  B ....
4 two computer games on the desk?
  ✘ (two CDs)
  A ....
  B ....
5 a jacket on the chair? ✘ (a T-shirt)
  A ....
  B ....
6 two windows in the room?
  ✔ (two small windows)
  A ....
  B ....

• Personal and object pronouns

6 Complete the sentences with personal and object pronouns.

1 Hey! That's my book! Give it to *me*!
2 David is my friend, and I like .... very much.
3 .... 'm Emilie and this is Celine. .... 're from France.
4 Is Naomi here? This book is for ....
5 That's Mr. Smith. .... 's a great English teacher.
6 That's a great song! Can I listen to .... ?
7 Hey, Vanessa! Where are they? I can't see ....
8 I have a sister. .... likes music.
9 Those are my dogs, Oscar and Ben. I love ....
10 I like blue. ....'s my favorite color.

• Possessive 's

7 Rewrite the sentences. Put apostrophes in the correct places.

1 It's my brothers birthday. He's sixteen.
  It's my brother's birthday. He's sixteen.
2 Lucy is Ralphs sister.
  ....
3 My cousins names are Patrick and Aaron.
  ....
4 These are Lauras bags.
  ....
5 Nicks father is a doctor.
  ....
6 That girls eyes are blue.
  ....
7 The childrens teacher is in the classroom.
  ....
8 The students backpacks are on the floor.
  ....

• Possessive adjectives

8 Rewrite the sentences with possessive adjectives.

1 My dad has a new book.
  His book is new.
2 I have white sneakers.
  ....
3 We have a nice teacher.
  ....
4 The cat has green eyes.
  ....
5 Maria's sister is a doctor.
  ....
6 You have a nice jacket.
  ....
7 Amy and Liam have a new computer.
  ....
8 I have a great magazine!
  ....

Vocabulary • Places

1 Look at the pictures. Complete the words.

park

m.......................

r.......................

l.......................

m.......................

c.......................

s.......................

z.......................

2 Choose the correct options.

1 Max and Emily are at the train *station*, but they don't have their tickets.
   a café   (b) station   c center

2 "I want a coffee and a sandwich."
   "Let's go to the .... ."
   a museum   b café   c library

3 I want to buy a T-shirt from the store in the .... .
   a library   b shopping mall   c station

4 There's a new swimming pool at the .... .
   a library   b movie theater   c gym

5 We want to see the elephants at the .... .
   a zoo   b museum   c shopping mall

6 In the .... you can play soccer.
   a library   b museum   c park

• Possessions

3 Complete the crossword.

Across

Down

• Countries and nationalities

4 Complete the puzzle and find the mystery country.

1 `B` `R` `I` `T` `A` `I` `N`
2
3
4
5
6
7
8
9

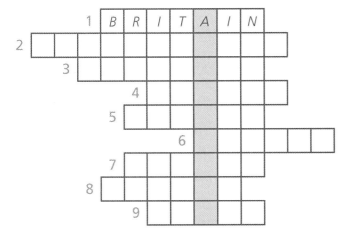

5 Complete the sentences.

1 Samantha is from Britain. She's *British*.
2 Kurt is from Germany. He's ....
3 Mandy is from the US. She's ....
4 Rosa is from Italy. She's ....
5 Vasily is from Russia. He's ....
6 Paulo is from Portugal. He's ....
7 Carmen is from Spain. She's ....
8 Alexis is from Greece. He's ....

6 Complete the text with these words.

| American | ~~fifteen~~ | France | gym |
| jeans | park | shopping | T-shirt |

Hi. My name's Sandrine, and I'm ¹ *fifteen* years old. I'm from ² ...., but my family and I don't live there. We live in New York, and I have a lot of ³ .... friends. I love New York. Our house is near a fantastic ⁴ ...., and there is also a ⁵ .... with a swimming pool.
That's me in the photo. Today I have my favorite ⁶ .... and blue ⁷ .... on. Do you like them? They're from a great store at my favorite ⁸ .... mall. New York is a great place for fashion!

Vocabulary • Sports

★ **1** Look at the pictures. Complete the crossword with the sports.

Across

Down

★ **2** Complete the sports.

1 ba $\underline{s}$ k $\underline{e}$ t b a $\underline{l}$ $\underline{l}$
2 s _ o _ b _ a _ d _ n g
3 m _ _ n _ _ _ n b _ k _ _ _
4 i _ e h _ c _ _ y
5 ic_ sk _ _ _ _ _
6 f _ _ _ b _ l _

★★ **3** Complete the text with *do*, *go* or *play*.

Adam and Vince ¹ *play* football every weekend. Their sister Judy doesn't ²........................ football—she doesn't like it—but she and her friends ³........................ tennis on Saturdays. They also ⁴........................ gymnastics at school, and they want to compete in the Olympic Games one day. During the Christmas holidays, Adam, Vince and Judy ⁵........................ snowboarding, and their parents ⁶........................ skiing. During the summer vacation they all ⁷........................ mountain biking. Next year the children want to start a new sport; Adam wants to ⁸........................ judo, Vince wants to ⁹........................ archery and Judy wants to ¹⁰........................ horseback riding.

★★★ **4** Write sentences with *do*, *go* and *play*.

1 we / swimming in the summer / judo in the winter
We go swimming in the summer and do judo in the winter.

2 Beth and Mark / basketball on Mondays / ice skating on the weekend
....

3 I / gymnastics at school / judo at home
....

4 they / horseback riding every day / tennis on Saturdays
....

5 Sam and Billy / judo / football at school
....

6 we / ice hockey in the winter / mountain biking in the summer
....

Workbook page 116

Reading

★ **(1)** **Look at the photo. Which sport is the interview about?**

   a Skiing   b Ice skating   c Ice hockey

Brain Trainer

Underline these words in the text:

1 Olympic sport   **4** other sports
2 easy   **5** swim
3 want   **6** night

Now do Exercise 2.

★ **(2)** **Read the interview. Answer the questions.**

  1 Is ice skating an Olympic sport?   *Yes, it is.*
  2 Is it an easy sport? ....
  3 What do Martin and Madeleine want to do one day? ....
  4 Do they do other sports? ....
  5 Can Martin swim? ....
  6 What time do Madeleine and Martin go to bed at night? ....

★★ **(3)** **Read the interview again. Are the statements true (T), false (F) or don't know (DK)?**

  1 Madeleine and Martin practice ice skating for two hours on school days.   *F*
  2 They practice ice skating once a day on the weekend. ....
  3 Martin likes his dance lessons. ....
  4 Madeleine talks about ice skating and two other sports. ....
  5 Martin doesn't like the ocean. ....
  6 Madeleine and Martin's friends do their homework before school. ....

★★ **(4)** **Complete the sentences.**

  1 Madeleine and Martin practice for *fifteen* hours a week on school days.
  2 They practice for .... hours every week.
  3 Good ice skaters can move well on the ice because they can ....
  4 In the mornings Madeleine and Martin have .... before they do their ....
  5 During vacation Madeleine goes ...., but Martin goes ....

Cool Sports!

In *Teen Sports* this week, James Biggs interviews twins Madeleine and Martin Rogers. Their favorite sport? Ice skating.

James	Madeleine, most young people do sports like track, swimming or tennis. Why is ice skating your favorite sport?
Madeleine	Because it's so beautiful.
James	But is it really a sport?
Martin	Yes, it's an Olympic sport, and it isn't easy! Madeleine and I practice every day after school for three hours. And on the weekend we practice for two hours in the morning and two hours in the evening. We want to win an Olympic medal one day.
Madeleine	We also have dance lessons once a week because ice skaters must move well on the ice.
James	Do you do any other sports?
Madeleine	Well, I do gymnastics at school, and on vacation I go swimming. I love the ocean, but Martin hates the water.
Martin	That's right. I can't swim, so I don't go with Madeleine. I go mountain biking instead.
James	So when do you find time to eat and sleep and do your homework?
Martin	It's difficult. We get up at five every morning—two hours before our friends! Then we have breakfast and do our homework before school.
Madeleine	We can't do our homework at night because we're tired. We go to bed at nine.
James	That's a long day! Well, thank you for speaking with me, and good luck in the next Olympics!

Grammar • Present simple

★ (1) **Choose the correct options.**

1 James *play* / *plays* basketball at school on Monday.
2 He *don't* / *doesn't* do judo every day.
3 *Do* / *Does* they go mountain biking on the weekend?
4 We *don't* / *doesn't* play tennis every Thursday.
5 What ball games does Julia *play* / *plays* at school?
6 I *watch* / *watches* football on TV.

★ (2) **Look at the table. Match the questions (1–6) with the answers (a–f).**

	Liam	Sarah	Melissa
go swimming	✓	✗	✗
play hockey	✓	✗	✓
go snowboarding	✓	✓	✓
do gymnastics	✗	✗	✗

1 Does Liam go snowboarding?   *d*
2 Do Sarah and Melissa do gymnastics?
3 Does Liam do gymnastics?
4 Does Sarah go snowboarding?
5 Do Liam and Melissa play hockey?
6 Does Sarah go swimming?

a No, he doesn't.
b Yes, she does.
c Yes, they do.
d Yes, he does.
e No, they don't.
f No, she doesn't.

★★ (3) **Look at the table in Exercise 2 again. Complete the sentences with the Present simple form of the verbs.**

1 Liam and Melissa *don't do* (do) gymnastics.
2 Melissa .... (play) hockey.
3 Sarah .... (go) swimming.
4 Liam and Sarah .... (go) snowboarding.
5 Sarah .... (do) gymnastics.
6 Sarah and Melissa .... (go) swimming.

★★ (4) **Write questions and answers in the Present simple.**

1 your friends / play / basketball after school? ✓
   A *Do your friends play basketball after school?*
   B *Yes, they do.*
2 you / go / mountain biking / on the weekend? ✗
   A ....
   B ....
3 your sister / like / team sports? ✓
   A ....
   B ....
4 you / play / a sport / on Fridays? ✓
   A ....
   B ....
5 your brother / watch TV / every day? ✗
   A ....
   B ....

★★★ (5) **Complete the email with the Present simple form of the verbs.**

New Message ⊗

Send

Hi Matt,
I ¹*love* (love) it here, and Helen ²......................
(love) it, too. We ³...................... (not want) to
go back to the US! Australia is a great country.
The weather is fantastic, and Helen and I
⁴...................... (go) swimming at the beach
every day. Mom and Dad ⁵......................
(come) with us, but Dad ⁶......................
(not go) in the water. He can't swim! What
⁷...................... (he / do)? Well, he
⁸...................... (sit) under an umbrella all day
and ⁹...................... (read) a newspaper!
Write soon,
James

Add Attachments: ⊗

• Verb + -ing

★ **6** Complete the sentences.

love: 😊😊 like/enjoy: 😊 don't mind: 😐
don't like: 😞 hate: 😞😞

1 Emma 😐 *doesn't mind* staying at home.
2 Cathy 😊 .... going running.
3 .... you 😊 ....
   watching the Olympic Games on TV?
4 I 😊😊 .... going skateboarding.
5 Andrea 😞😞 .... swimming.
6 Dad 😐 .... watching baseball.
7 I 😞 .... getting up early.
8 .... Eddie 😐 ....
   playing basketball?

★★ **7** Complete the sentences with the **-ing** form of the verbs.

1 We love *watching* (watch) football games on TV.
2 They don't like .... (do) judo
   at school.
3 Why does Amy hate .... (play)
   ice hockey?
4 The boys don't mind .... (take)
   me with them to the gym.
5 Do you enjoy .... (swim)
   in cold water?
6 Mom doesn't like .... (go)
   horseback riding.

★★ **8** Write sentences.

1 Helen and Nick / 😊 / play / tennis
   Helen and Nick like playing tennis.
2 my brother / 😊😊 / watch /
   the Olympic Games / on TV!
   ....
3 we / 😞😞 / swim / in the ocean
   ....
4 Sonia / 😐 / practice / every day
   ....
5 David / 😊 / snowboarding / in winter?
   ....
6 I / 😞 / do / my homework / on the weekend
   ....

Grammar Reference pages 108–109

Vocabulary • Compound nouns

★ **1** Match 1–6 to a–f to make compound nouns.

1 soccer   a skates
2 tennis   b stick
3 hockey   c racket
4 judo   d suit
5 ice   e belt
6 swim   f cleats

★ **2** Complete the sentences with these words.

~~court~~ court field pool rink

1 I play basketball on the basketball *court*.
2 She doesn't like swimming at the swimming
   ....
3 Do you go ice skating at the new ice skating
   .... ?
4 We play football on the football ....
5 He plays tennis on this tennis ....

★★ **3** Complete the sentences with these words.

~~cleats~~ court judo stick swimsuit tennis

1 You have soccer practice after school.
   Please take your soccer *cleats* with you.
2 She is swimming in the ocean.
   She's wearing a blue ....
3 I don't have a .... racket.
4 What color .... belt do you have?
5 You can't play ice hockey! You don't have
   a hockey ....
6 There are ten players on the basketball
   ....

★★ **4** Complete the text.

On Mondays Rachel plays ice hockey, and she
takes her [1] *hockey stick* with her. On Wednesdays
she does judo. She's very good, and she has a
green [2] .... On Fridays she does
gymnastics, and she practices at the [3] ....
On Saturday mornings she puts on her tennis
clothes. Then she takes her [4] .... and
goes to the [5] .... In the afternoons
she goes ice skating at the [6] ....
She loves this sport.

Workbook page 116

Chatroom Opinions

Speaking and Listening

★ **1** Complete the sentences with these words.

> do   favorite   ~~it~~   like   of   think

1 I can't play tennis! That's *it*! I quit!
2 What do you think .... my new tennis racket?
3 Mrs. Marshall is my .... teacher.
4 I don't .... going to the ice skating rink. It's boring.
5 I .... Usain Bolt is amazing.
6 .... you like watching the Olympic Games on TV?

★ **2** Match the questions (1–5) to the answers (a–e).
1.2 Then listen and check.

1 What do you think of Boston?   *c*
2 Do you like watching archery?
3 What do you think of Usain Bolt?
4 Do you like Rihanna?
5 What do you think of the Bulls?

a He's my favorite athlete. I think he's amazing!
b I think they're good, but the Thunder is my favorite team.
c Well, I think the weather is terrible, but I like the people.
d Yes, I do. I think it's an amazing sport.
e No, I don't. Beyoncé is my favorite singer.

★★ **3** Complete the conversation with these phrases.
1.3 Then listen and check.

> Do you like   ~~Good idea~~
> I don't like   I love
> I think   Nadal is my favorite player
> What do you think

Carlos	Do you want to watch tennis on TV?
Zak	[1] *Good idea!*
Carlos	What about you, Nadia?
Nadia	Sorry, Carlos. [2] .... tennis is boring.
Carlos	Really? I love it. [3] .... of Novak Djokovic, Zak?
Zak	I think he's great, but [4] ....
Jody	My favorite sport is horseback riding. I go horseback riding every weekend.
Zak	[5] .... horses, Nadia?
Nadia	Yes, I do. [6] .... them. I can't ride, but I want to learn.
Jody	Do you? What about you, Zak?
Zak	No, thanks! [7] .... horses.

★★ **4** Read the conversation in Exercise 3 again. Are the statements true (T), false (F) or don't know (DK)?

1 Zak wants to watch tennis with Carlos.   *T*
2 Nadia doesn't like tennis.   ....
3 Roger Federer is Jody's favorite player.   ....
4 Jody likes horseback riding.   ....
5 Nadia goes horseback riding every weekend.   ....
6 Zak doesn't want to go horseback riding.   ....

★★ **5** Look at the table and write a conversation between Andy and Eva. Use the information below and expressions from Exercise 3.

	Likes	Doesn't like
Andy	playing football listening to music watching TV	reading books shopping cooking
Eva	swimming reading books playing computer games	watching TV getting up early cooking

Speaking and Listening page 120

Grammar • Adverbs of frequency

★ **1** **Complete the table with these adverbs of frequency.**

| always | hardly ever | ~~never~~ |
| often | ~~sometimes~~ | usually |

☆☆☆☆ *never*
★☆☆☆ _____
★★☆☆ *sometimes* / _____
★★★☆ _____
★★★★ _____

Brain Trainer

Draw pictures to help you remember words.
1 ⚽⚽⚽ *usually*
2 ⚽ *hardly ever*
Now do Exercise 2.

★ **2** **Look at the table. Complete the sentences.**

	Naomi	Jake	Harry	Isobel
go swimming on Tuesdays	🚗🚗🚗	–	🚗🚗🚗🚗	🚗🚗🚗🚗
do homework after school	📚📚📚📚	📚📚	–	📚
watch TV on the weekend	📺	📺📺	📺	–

1 Naomi *usually* goes swimming on Tuesdays.
2 Harry .... does his homework after school.
3 Harry and Naomi .... watch TV on the weekend.
4 Isobel .... goes swimming on Tuesdays.
5 Jake and Isobel .... do their homework after school.
6 Jake .... goes swimming on Tuesdays.
7 Isobel .... watches TV on the weekend.

Grammar Reference pages 108–109

★★ **3** **Rewrite the sentences with the adverbs of frequency in the correct place.**

1 We play tennis on Saturday afternoons. (always)
We always play tennis on Saturday afternoons.
2 Julia goes skateboarding with her friends on the weekend. (sometimes)
....
....
3 I meet my friends at the gym after school. (often)
....
....
4 I wear a basketball shirt at home. (hardly ever)
....
....
5 Sam takes his tennis racket to school. (never)
....
....
6 I am happy on the weekend. (usually)
....
....

★★ **4** **Write sentences and questions.**

1 we / always / not get up / late on the weekend
We don't always get up late on the weekend.
2 I / sometimes / be / tired / in the evening
....
3 he / often / cook / dinner / for his family?
....
4 our teacher / hardly ever / give / us / tests
....
5 you / usually / meet / your friends / after school?
....
6 I / not / always / watch / football / on Sundays
....

★★★ **5** **Answer the questions.**

1 What do you always do in the evening?
I always listen to music.
2 What do you and your friends usually do on the weekend?
....
3 What do you sometimes do on vacation?
....
4 What sports do you hardly ever watch on TV?
....
5 What do you never do?
....

Reading

1 **Read the article quickly. Find:**

1 one country   *France*
2 two people   ....
3 a movie   ....
4 four sports   ....
5 two places in a town   ....

IT'S FAST,
IT'S EXCITING—
IT'S FREE RUNNING!

Free running is an exciting new sport from France, but it has fans all over the world. You don't usually see free runners on tracks. You see them in the street or in parks. They climb walls, jump from building to building and do a lot of other amazing movements. It is important to move fast, but it is also important to move beautifully.

Good free runners practice every day. They don't wear special clothes, but good running shoes are important. Free runners sometimes run with their MP3 players and listen to their favorite music.

Free running is a difficult sport, but it's very popular with teenagers. Free runner Robbie Dowling, 17, says, "Free running is different from sports like track, football or judo. When I go free running, I don't want to win or lose; I just want to have fun. Sure, there are competitions, but they aren't important to me or my friends. We don't take part in them."

For other young people, free running competitions are important, and you can watch some amazing videos on YouTube. You can also watch Sébastien Foucan, the man who started the sport, free running in the James Bond movie *Casino Royale*. Sébastien says that free runners practice all the time. He also says there is no good or bad in free running, but it is important to learn from your experiences.

2 **Read the article again. Choose the correct options.**

1 People all over the world (enjoy) / don't enjoy free running.
2 Free runners usually practice *in the street* / *on a track*.
3 *All* / *Some* free runners practice every day.
4 Free runners don't wear *special shoes* / *special clothes*.
5 Robbie Dowling *wants to win* / *doesn't enter* free running competitions.
6 You can watch free running competitions *on YouTube* / *in the movie* Casino Royale.

3 **Complete the summary with words from the article.**

Free running is a sport with [1] *fans* all over the world. Free runners usually run in the [2] .... or in parks. Some people go free running because they want to have [3] .... Other people like taking part in [4] ...., but there is no good or [5] .... in free running. It's a great sport!

Listening

1 **Listen to the radio show about sports clothes.**
1.4 **Mark the words you hear.**

gym   ☐
soccer shirts   ☐
soccer cleats   ☐
ice hockey   ☐
tennis racket   ☐
running shoes   ☐

2 **Listen again. Choose the correct options.**
1.4
1 Mark (always) / sometimes wears soccer shirts.
2 He *likes* / *doesn't like* playing soccer.
3 *Soccer* / *Ice hockey* is Mark's favorite sport.
4 Elena *loves* / *hates* wearing running shoes.
5 She *always* / *never* wears soccer shirts.

Writing • A description of a sport

1 Match 1–5 to a–e.

1 comma ———— a !
2 period   b '
3 question mark   c ,
4 apostrophe   d ?
5 exclamation point   e .

2 Put the correct punctuation in the sentences.

1 *At school, we play football, basketball and tennis.*
2 Do you enjoy playing tennis with your friends
3 I dont like watching ice hockey on TV, but I love playing it
4 Lionel Messi is an amazing player He's great
5 This is Lucys sisters judo belt
6 Are there ten or eleven players on a soccer team

3 Read the text. Match the questions (1–3) to the paragraphs (A–C).

1 What's my favorite sport at school?   ....
2 What do I think of sports at school?   ....
3 What sports are there at school?   *A.*

4 Think about sports at your school. Complete the sentences.

1 Sports at school are ....
2 At my school, there's ....
3 My favorite sport is ....
4 We play ....
5 I think sports at school are ....

5 Write a description of sports at your school. Use the paragraph guide from Exercise 3 and your sentences from Exercise 4.

....
....
....
....
....
....
....
....
....
....
....

Sports at School

A Sports at my school are amazing. There's tennis, basketball, football and track. We sometimes go swimming in the swimming pool. My friends love tennis, and they play every day. I hardly ever play tennis because I don't like it. I think it's difficult.

B My favorite sport is basketball. I think it's an exciting sport, and I play on the school basketball team. We play basketball every Monday and Wednesday, and there are games every week. We aren't very good and we usually lose, but we have fun!

C I think sports at school are great. I love playing on a team with my friends. It's never boring.

The Big Picture

Vocabulary • Types of movies

★ **1** **Complete the movie words.**

1 h o r r o r m o v i e
2 m _ _ i _ a _
3 d _ _ u _ e _ t _ r _
4 a _ t _ _ n m _ v _ _
5 _ _ m _ d _
6 s _ _ _ _ _ e f _ _ _ _ o _ _ _ vie
7 f _ _ _ _ _ y
8 m _ _ _ ial a _ _ _ m _ _ ie
9 a _ _ m _ t _ _ _
10 we _ _ e _ _
11 w _ r _ _ vie
12 h _ _ t _ _ ic _ _ _ _ vie

★★ **2** **Complete the sentences with the correct movie words.**

1 This is Dan's favorite *comedy*. He loves the jokes.
2 I don't like this m .... The songs are boring.
3 The alien and the boy are friends. It's a good s .... f .... m ....
4 We're making an a .... Look at my cartoons!
5 The d .... is about snakes. It's interesting and I'm learning a lot.
6 The m .... a .... m .... was good. I love judo and karate!

Workbook page 117

★★ **3** **Write sentences.**

1 she / like / action movies
She likes action movies.
2 we / not enjoy / horror movies
....
3 I / not like / this documentary
....
4 you / watch / musicals?
....
5 he / never / watch / animations
....
6 they / not like / science fiction movies
....

★★★ **4** **Complete the text with these words.**

| comedies | historical movies | horror movies |
| musicals | ~~science fiction movies~~ | westerns |

My family and I love going to the movie theater, but we don't like the same kinds of movies. Mom likes [1] *science fiction movies* because she loves stories about the future. Dad is a fan of [2] .... He enjoys scary stories about vampires. My little sister likes [3] .... ! She says she likes stories about cowboys, but I think she watches these movies because there are usually horses in them. She loves horses. I like [4] .... because I like laughing, and I love [5] .... because the songs in them are often great. I also enjoy [6] .... about kings and queens.

Reading

Brain Trainer

Look at the pictures. They often help you understand a text.
Now do Exercise 1.

★ **(1)** Read the magazine article quickly. Match the people (1–5) to the pictures (a–e).

1 Anna   .d.
2 Frank   ....
3 Rachel   ....
4 Tanya   ....
5 Tom   ....

Fantastic Film Club

The best club for thirteen- to sixteen-year-olds at our school is the Film Club. It has fifty-one members, and we meet every Saturday. We usually watch movies together and talk about them afterward. What do we watch? Comedies, action movies, historical movies, war movies and many other types of movies. I like fantasies and *The Lord of the Rings* movies are my favorites.

Every year the members of the club do a big project. This year we are doing something special: we're making a musical about a school in New York.

Today is Saturday, January 16, and we're all at the club. We're working hard because we want to start filming in two months. Rachel and Tom are over there. Rachel is writing the music for the musical. Her job is difficult because there are a lot of songs in the musical. Tom is next to her. He's writing the story for the movie, and he and Rachel work together. They're important people in this project.

What are the other people doing? Well, Anna is doing the special effects. In the story, there's a storm in New York, and Anna is making storm noises on her computer. Are the actors acting? No, they aren't. They're listening to Tanya. She's singing one of Rachel's songs, and Frank is playing the piano. They're amazing. This is going to be a great musical!

★ **(2)** Read the text again. Choose the correct options.

1 The members of the Film Club do a project every *year* / *Saturday*.
2 They often *watch* / *make* movies and talk about them.
3 The writer's favorite movies are *musicals* / *fantasies*.
4 The members want to start *writing* / *filming* the musical in two months.
5 The writer *likes* / *doesn't like* Tanya's singing.

★★ **(3)** Match the sentence beginnings (1–6) to the endings (a–f).

1 About fifty people are   f
2 The writer's favorite movies are
3 This year the Film Club is making a movie about
4 Tom and Rachel are important because they are writing
5 The actors are listening to
6 The writer thinks Frank is

a the story and the music.
b a school in New York.
c fantasies.
d a good piano player.
e one of Rachel's songs.
f in the Film Club.

★★★ **(4)** Answer the questions.

1 What do the club members usually do on Saturdays?
   They usually watch movies and talk about them afterward.
2 What do they do every year?
   ....
   ....
3 What do they want to do in March?
   ....
   ....
4 Why is Rachel's job difficult?
   ....
   ....
5 What kind of special effects is Anna doing at the moment?
   ....
   ....

Grammar • Present continuous

★ (1) **Complete the sentences with the Present continuous form of the verbs.**

1 Sylvia *is watching* (watch) TV.
2 The boys .... (dance) in the musical.
3 We .... tennis (not play) at the moment.
4 He .... (swim) in the pool.
5 I .... (study) for a test right now.
6 She .... (not look) at us.
7 I .... (not wait) for Anna.
   I .... (wait) for Mike.

★ (2) **Choose the correct options.**

1 Are / Is they writing songs? Yes, they are / is.
2 Are / Is Ben acting? No, he aren't / isn't.
3 Are / Is you making a movie? Yes, I am / are.
4 Are / Is we buying the tickets? No, we aren't / isn't.
5 Are / Is they studying? No, they aren't / isn't.

★★ (3) **Look at the picture. Make sentences with the Present continuous.**

1 Amy / not sing – she / dance
   Amy isn't singing. She's dancing.
2 Jake / not run – he / sit
   ....
3 Billy and Leona / not watch Amy – they / talk
   ....
4 Kate and Anna / not laugh – they / dance
   ....
5 the / director / not smile – she / watch / Ben
   ....
6 Lucy / not talk / to the director – she / talk / on her cell phone
   ....
   ....

Grammar Reference pages 110–111

★★ (4) **Look at the picture again. Make questions and answers.**

1 what / Ben / do?
   What is Ben doing? He's running.
2 Amy / study?
   ....
3 Billy and Leona / sing?
   ....
4 Lucy / laugh?
   ....
5 what / Jake / do?
   ....
6 who / the director / watch?
   ....

★★★ (5) **Imagine you are at home with your family in the evening. What are you and your family doing? Write five sentences.**

I'm not watching TV. I'm doing my homework. Mom isn't …

KATE   ANNA   AMY   BEN

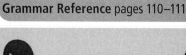

JAKE

LEONA   BILLY   LUCY   DIRECTOR

Vocabulary • Adjectives

★ **1** Find twelve adjectives.

E	S	I	D	V	X	G	A	D	Y	N
C	T	A	G	F	U	N	N	Y	R	F
I	E	H	D	J	L	I	L	E	A	Z
T	R	T	A	S	T	Y	E	X	C	Q
N	R	S	U	A	Y	O	B	C	S	W
A	I	E	X	P	E	N	S	I	V	E
M	B	B	O	R	I	N	G	T	C	I
O	L	T	E	I	N	A	D	I	S	R
R	E	R	I	L	W	I	A	N	T	D
E	M	O	S	E	W	A	R	G	D	H

★ **2** Match these words to the pictures.

annoying	boring	exciting
~~expensive~~	romantic	terrible

expensive

....

....

....

....

....

★★ **3** Put the letters in the correct order.

1 Max loves telling jokes. He's *funny*.   nunfy
2 This ice cream is great.
   It's very ....   ttsay
3 I love this movie! It's .... !   moseeaw
4 I don't understand the story.
   It's ....   edrwi
5 The horror movie is about zombies.
   It's ....   arsyc
6 People always cry when they watch the movie.
   It's very ....   dsa

★★ **4** Complete the text with adjectives from Exercise 1. More than one option is possible for some spaces.

It's Saturday evening. Charlie and his family want to see a movie. They don't want to go to the movie theater because the tickets are [1] *expensive*. They want to eat some [2] .... pizza and watch a DVD, but which one? The action movie is [3] ...., but Charlie doesn't want to watch it again. He wants to watch a [4] .... movie, but his mom and dad don't like comedies. Charlie's dad says the war film is [5] ...., and he wants to watch it, but Charlie's mom says it's [6] .... The horror movie is good, but it's very [7] ...., and Charlie's little sister is only five. There's a documentary about animals, but Charlie's grandma doesn't want to watch it. She says documentaries are [8] ....

Workbook page 117

Chatroom Suggestions

Speaking and Listening

★ **1** **Put the words in the correct order.**

1 **A** (we / don't / later / Why / go / to the movies / ?)
Why don't we go to the movies later?

B (way / No / !) *No way!* I have a test tomorrow.

2 **A** (a / Let's / horror movie / watch)
....

B (in / I'm / !) .... I love horror movies.

3 **A** (How / computer game / playing / this / about / ?)
....

B (idea / That / good / 's / a) .... I love games like this.

★ **2** **Complete the conversations with these words.**
1.5 **Then listen and check.**

about	don't	~~go~~	going
I'm	let's	way	why

1 **A** Let's [1] *go* for a walk in the park.
B No, thanks! It's raining!
2 **A** [2] .... don't we go for a walk in the park?
B That's a good idea. It's a beautiful day.
3 **A** How about [3] .... for a walk in the park?
B [4] .... in! We can go skateboarding there.
4 **A** [5] .... make dinner for Mom and Dad tonight.
B That's a good idea.
5 **A** What [6] .... making dinner for Mom and Dad tonight?
B No [7] .... ! I can't cook!
6 **A** Why [8] .... we make dinner for Mom and Dad tonight?
B OK. We can make them some chicken.

Speaking and Listening page 121

★★ **3** **Complete the conversation with these phrases.**
1.6 **Then listen and check.**

a good idea	I'm in	let's see
no, thanks	how about meeting	~~why don't we~~

Carlos What are you doing, Nadia?
Nadia I'm reading a book about old movies. It's interesting.
Jody Well, [1] *why don't we* go to the movies? *Casablanca* is playing at Movieland.
Nadia Great! [2] .... !
Zak *Casablanca?*
Nadia It's an old black-and-white movie. It's very romantic!
Zak [3] .... ! Those movies are boring!
Carlos Zak's right. [4] .... the new comedy.
Jody Well, [5] .... outside the movie theater? You and Zak can see the comedy, and Nadia and I can see *Casablanca*.
Carlos That's [6] ....

★★ **4** **Read the conversation in Exercise 3 again. Answer the questions.**

1 Why is Nadia reading a book about old movies?
It's interesting.
2 Does Zak know what type of movie *Casablanca* is?
....
3 What is Zak's opinion of old black-and-white movies?
....
4 What does Carlos want to see?
....
5 What does Carlos think of Jody's suggestion?
....

★★★ **5** **You and your friends want to do something interesting today. Write a conversation and make suggestions. You can use your own ideas or the ideas below.**

You	go to the beach / play tennis
Friend 1	go to the swimming pool / go to the movies
Friend 2	go skiing / have a party

Grammar • Present simple and Present continuous

★ **1** **Complete the sentences with the Present simple or Present continuous form of the verbs.**

1 I *usually take* (usually / take) black-and-white photographs, but at the moment I *am taking* (take) color pictures.
2 Anna .... (usually / not make) documentaries. This year she .... (work) on a horror movie.
3 You .... (usually / read) a book on the bus, but today you .... (not read). You .... (listen) to your MP3 player.
4 Emily and Alice .... (usually / not read) sports magazines, but today they .... (read) about football. They .... (not read) about music.
5 Mark .... (usually / work) in his dad's store after school, but this afternoon he .... (not help) his dad. He .... (play) tennis with his friends.
6 We .... (usually / have) a dance class on Fridays, but this Friday we .... (watch) a DVD at my house.

★ **2** **Match the questions (1–10) to the answers (a–j).**

1 Is Tessa working in her mom's store today?   *e*
2 Does Jimmy take photos with his phone?
3 Are you and your friend doing your homework?
4 Do the friends often go to the movies?
5 Are you watching the horror movie on TV?
6 Do you and Nick always play tennis together?
7 Does Tessa help her mother in the store?
8 Is Jimmy taking photographs of the people at the party?
9 Do you often watch DVDs at home?
10 Are your parents having breakfast?

a No, he isn't.
b Yes, we are.
c No, I don't.
d Yes, I am.
e Yes, she is.
f No, they don't.
g Yes, he does.
h Yes, we do.
i Yes, they are.
j Yes, she does.

★★ **3** **Complete the text with the Present simple or Present continuous form of the verbs.**

Hi Anna,
I'm in Paris at a school for dancers, and I [1] *'m having* (have) a great time! I usually [2] .... (go) to dance classes in the morning, but today is Saturday, and I [3] .... (sit) in a café in Montmartre and [4] .... (write) this postcard.
On weekends I sometimes [5] .... (meet) my French friends in the evening, and we [6] .... (watch) a good movie at the movie theater. My best friend here is Emilie, and we often [7] .... (do) things together, but at the moment she [8] .... (visit) her grandma.
Write soon,
Samantha

★★ **4** **Make sentences in the Present simple and Present continuous.**

1 She usually / work / in a café after school / but / she / do / her homework / today
She usually works in a café after school, but she is doing her homework today.
2 I / often / take / photographs / but / I / not use / my camera / right now
....
3 Alice / hardly ever / do / sports / but / she / do / gymnastics / at the moment
....
4 Lucy / usually / sit / with Adam / but / she / sit / with me / today
....
5 our cousins / sometimes / visit / us / on the weekend / but today / we / visit them
....

★★★ **5** **Make sentences.**

1 usually / at the moment
I usually do my homework after school, but I'm watching TV at the moment.
I ....
2 every day / today
My friends ....
3 sometimes / now
Mom and Dad ....

Grammar Reference pages 110–111

Reading

Brain Trainer

Don't answer the questions too quickly! Sometimes all the answer options are in the text. So read the text carefully!
Now do Exercise 1.

1 Read the festival blog quickly. Where is Anke from?

a the US   b Germany   c Japan

HOME   NEWS   BLOG   FEATURES

International Student Film Festival!

Today is the beginning of the International Student Film Festival in Rome, and it's an exciting day for the young people here. There are students from the United States, Europe and Japan. One of them is Anke Müller, from Germany. Anke is a seventeen-year-old student, and she's staying with friends in Italy this summer. She's taking part in the festival for the first time.

"Animations are my favorite, and I love the Wallace and Gromit movies," she says. "Some of the characters in these movies are really weird, but they're all awesome, and Gromit, the dog, is very funny."

Anke loves watching movies, and she also makes animations about funny people. "I love watching people in the street, in the park, at school," she says. "They often do weird things."

Anke makes her movies at home. "My film studio is my bedroom," she says. "I sit there every day, and I make the scenes and characters." It isn't always easy for Anke. "I don't have a lot of free time because I often have a lot of homework. I love making movies, but I don't always like doing my homework!"

This festival is great for Anke because she's here with new friends. They can watch movies and talk to movie directors. Anke's favorite movie at the festival is a science fiction movie called *The Robot Returns*. "It's very scary," says Anke, "but the special effects are amazing."

2 Read the blog again. Answer the questions.

1 How old is Anke?
She's seventeen years old.
2 Where is she staying this summer?
....
3 What is her opinion of the characters in the Wallace and Gromit movies?
....
4 What kind of movie does she make?
....
5 What are her movies about?
....
6 What is Anke's favorite movie at the festival?
....

3 Complete the summary with words from the article.

Anke Müller is a student. She [1] *is staying* with friends in Italy this summer, and she [2] .... in a film festival in Rome. Anke loves watching movies, and she also [3] .... animations about funny people. It isn't easy because she doesn't usually have a lot of [4] .... Her favorite movie at the festival is a science fiction movie. Anke thinks the [5] .... in this movie are very good.

Listening

1 Read the message. Then listen to Laura and Adam.
1.7 Who is going to the movies? Mark the correct option.

a Laura ....   b Adam ....

HI FROM
MOVIE WORLD!
....
Get your free tickets for
The Robot Returns on
Saturday.
Call now at (212) 546-....

2 Listen again. Are the statements
1.7 true (T), false (F) or don't know (DK)?

1 Adam got a text message from Movie World. *F*
2 Laura doesn't usually watch action movies. ....
3 Laura wants to see the movie on Sunday. ....
4 Adam plays basketball on Sunday. ....
5 Kate wants to go to the movies with Laura. ....

Writing • A movie review

1 Read the movie review. Find *and, but* and *because*.

StreetDance 3D – A Great Movie!

(A) I love the movie **StreetDance 3D**. It's a musical and a love story. I like watching the DVD with my friends because we're students at a dance school.

(B) *StreetDance 3D* is about a group of young dancers. In the movie, they are practicing for a big dance contest. The group loses an important dancer, but they don't stop practicing. They want to win.

(C) The movie has interesting characters. My favorite is Carly because she is funny and she can dance. I also like Helena, a teacher at a ballet school. Eddie is another great character. He's an awesome dancer. All dancers wear cool clothes, and the special effects are amazing.

(D) I think *StreetDance 3D* is a great movie because the story is exciting and the music is special.

2 Complete the sentences with *and, but* or *because*.

1 I like the movie *because* it has great music.
2 The special effects are good, ... the actors are terrible.
3 We want to go shopping .... meet our friends on Saturday morning.
4 She can't make dinner .... she can't cook.
5 I often go to the gym, ... I never play basketball there.
6 I don't like the musical .... the story is weird, ... the songs are good.

3 Read the review again. Answer the questions.

1 What kind of movie is it?
....
2 What is it about?
....
3 What is good in the movie?
....
4 Do you want to watch it?
....

4 Think about a movie you like. Answer the questions.

1 What is the name of the movie? What kind of movie is it?
....
2 Who do you watch the movie with?
....
3 What is it about?
....
4 What characters are in the movie?
....
5 What is good in the movie?
....
6 Why do you think the movie is great?
....

5 Write a movie review. Use the paragraph guide from Exercise 3 and your notes from Exercise 4 to help you.

....
....
....
....

3 Past Lives

Vocabulary • History

Brain Trainer

Draw a history word. It helps you remember it!

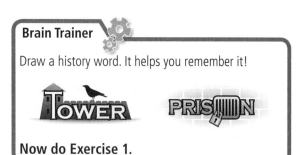

Now do Exercise 1.

★ (1) **Look at the pictures. Complete the crossword.**

Across

Down

★ (2) **Choose the correct options.**

1 The *dungeon* / *prisoner* was a cold and dark place.
2 The *army* / *castle* was big with strong walls.
3 Please don't *die* / *kill* that animal!
4 They don't clean the house or cook. They have *servants* / *soldiers*.
5 King Edward III of England lived in the fourteenth *century* / *plague*.
6 When did the Second World *Sword* / *War* start?

★★ (3) **Complete the sentences with these words.**

castle	century	knight	plague
prisoner	servants	soldiers	war

1 A *century* is a hundred years.
2 There are thousands of .... in an army.
3 Their .... do all the work in the house.
4 The king put the .... in the dungeon.
5 The king and queen live in a ....
6 In a .... , thousands of people die.
7 The .... has a big horse and a sword.
8 The .... is a terrible disease.

★★ (4) **Complete the text with these words.**

army	century	dying
killing	plague	queen

It is the fourteenth [1] *century*. The king and [2] .... are in the castle. The servants are bringing them food and drink. But outside, things are not good. There is a terrible war between the English and the French, and the [3] .... of the English king is in France. Thousands of people are [4] .... in this war, and there is also a [5] .... in Europe. This disease is [6] .... both rich and poor people.

Workbook page 118

Reading

★ **(1)** **Read the text quickly. Choose the best title.**

a The Story of Merlin
b The Story of King Arthur
c The Story of Queen Guinevere

★ **(2)** **Read the text again. Choose the correct options.**

1 *Uther Pendragon* / *Sir Ector* was Arthur's father.
2 *Uther Pendragon* / *Sir Ector* took care of Arthur when he was a child.
3 Arthur became king because he pulled a sword out of *the ground* / *a stone*.
4 Arthur made a round table for *Guinevere* / *his knights*.
5 Guinevere went to France with *Lancelot* / *Arthur*.
6 Arthur *died* / *didn't die* in the war.

★★ **(3)** **Are the statements true (T), false (F) or don't know (DK)?**

1 Arthur's mother was Igraine of Cornwall.   *T*
2 Sir Ector took Merlin away from his parents when he was a baby.   ....
3 Arthur was eighteen years old when Uther died.   ....
4 The table was round because there were many knights.   ....
5 Arthur's knights all liked him.   ....
6 The war started because Mordred tried to take the kingdom from Arthur.   ....

★★ **(4)** **Complete the sentences.**

1 Arthur's parents were Uther and *Igraine*.
2 Uther died when Arthur was a .... man.
3 The name of Arthur's .... was Camelot.
4 Lancelot was the best........................in Camelot.
5 Mordred started a ...., and many knights died.

Arthur was the son of King Uther Pendragon and Igraine of Cornwall. When he was a baby, Merlin, the magician, took him away from his parents, and he lived with a kind knight, Sir Ector. The years passed. Arthur became a young man and Uther died. There was no king in England.

Then, one day, a stone came out of the ground with a sword in it. Merlin said to the people, "Pull the sword out of the stone and you can be king." Many people tried, but only Arthur pulled out the sword. He became king!

Arthur built a castle called Camelot, and he married Guinevere. Many knights came to Camelot, and Arthur made a round table for them. The table was round to show that all the knights were equal. But they weren't really equal; the best knight was Sir Lancelot.

Lancelot and Queen Guinevere fell in love. They went to France, and Arthur followed them. Arthur's son, Mordred, stayed in England. Arthur asked him to take care of the country. But Mordred hated Arthur, and he tried to take Arthur's country away from him. There was a war, and most of the Knights of the Round Table died. But Arthur didn't die. Three queens took him to Avalon. Some people think that Arthur is not dead now. They think he lives in Avalon today!

Grammar • Past simple: affirmative and negative

★ 1 Choose the correct options.

Alice and Jake Williams ¹ *was /* (*were*) at the castle yesterday. Their parents, Mr. and Mrs. Williams, ² *wasn't / weren't* with them. They ³ *was / were* at home. The castle ⁴ *wasn't / weren't* very big, and it ⁵ *wasn't / weren't* interesting. There ⁶ *was / were* a dungeon, but there ⁷ *wasn't / weren't* prisoners in the dungeon. There ⁸ *was / were* hundreds of people at the castle, but these people ⁹ *wasn't / weren't* kings, queens or knights. It ¹⁰ *was / were* boring!

★ 2 Complete the sentences with the Past simple form of these verbs.

come	do	give	have	meet
not stay	not visit	~~read~~	send	take

1 I *read* the book last year in school.
2 We .... dinner an hour ago.
3 Karen .... me an email yesterday.
4 Oscar and Matt .... to my house yesterday.
5 He .... in a hotel.
6 They .... their friends outside the movie theater.
7 Mom .... the dog for a walk in the park.
8 She .... her little brother a toy sword for his birthday.
9 They .... the museum.
10 They .... their homework and went to bed.

★★ 3 Complete the email with the Past simple form of the verbs.

New Message

Hi Ben,
How are you? I ¹ *had* (have) a great weekend. On Saturday I ² .... (go) mountain biking with friends. We ³ .... (visit) an old castle in the countryside. It ⁴ .... (be) interesting, but we ⁵ .... (not see) any ghosts! In the afternoon, my friend Emma ⁶ .... (come) to my house. We ⁷ .... (watch) a new DVD about monsters. Emma ⁸ .... (not like) it because she hates scary movies!
Talk to you soon,
Samantha

Send

★★ 4 Complete the story with the Past simple form of these verbs.

eat	feel	~~go~~	have	not go
not listen	say	stay	watch	

Last night Ursula's parents ¹ *went* to the movies. Ursula ² .... with them. She ³ .... at home. "Be good and go to sleep early," her mother ⁴ ....
But Ursula ⁵ .... to her mother. She ⁶ .... a horror movie on TV. At midnight she ⁷ .... hungry, so she ⁸ .... pizza and ice cream. That night she ⁹ .... a bad dream.

Grammar Reference pages 112–113

Vocabulary • Life events

★ **1** Match these words to the pictures.

die	fall in love	graduate
have a baby	retire	~~start school~~

start school

....

....

....

....

....

★ **2** Choose the correct options.

1 *have / get* a baby
2 *have / be* born
3 *go / get* married
4 *go / have* to college
5 *leave / have* home
6 *be / find* a job
7 *leave / get* school

★★ **3** Match the beginnings (1–5) to the endings (a–e).

1 Maria and Manuel got   *d*
2 Natasha and Ivan had
3 Maurice fell in
4 Grandpa left
5 I found

a a baby last month.
b a job in a clothing store.
c love with Claudette.
d married last year.
e school when he was seventeen.

★★ **4** Complete the sentences with the Past simple form of these verbs.

be born	~~get married~~	graduate
move	retire	start school

1 My parents fell in love when they were in college and *got married* five years later.
2 Alex .... with high grades from a very good college.
3 Beth .... six months ago, but she still can't read!
4 Mr. Evans .... when he was sixty-six years old. Now he stays at home and works in his garden.
5 I .... on July 4, 2002.
6 We lived downtown for many years, but we .... a year ago.

★★ **5** Complete the text with the Past simple form of these verbs.

~~be born~~	be born	fall in love
find a job	get married	leave home
leave school	retire	start school

Mark Jones [1] *was born* in 1915, and he [2] .... when he was six. Mark didn't like studying, and he [3] .... ten years later. He [4] .... in a clothing store. One day a pretty girl named Ivy Brown came into the store to buy something. Mark [5] .... with her, and they [6] .... in 1937. Their first baby, Eliza, [7] .... two years later. Mark, Ivy and Eliza were very happy together. The years passed. Eliza grew up and [8] .... Mark and Ivy became grandparents. Mark [9] .... when he was seventy. He died fifteen years later, and Ivy died a month after Mark.

Workbook page 118

Chatroom Reasoning

Speaking and Listening

★ **1** Complete the conversations
1.8 with these words. Then listen and check.

because	because	not
silly	~~why~~	why

1 **A** *Why* do you want to go to the park?
   B .... we can go skateboarding there.
2 **A** Let's go to the park this afternoon.
   B Don't be .... ! It's snowing.
3 **A** I don't want to go for a walk.
   B Why .... ? It's a nice day. Come on!
4 **A** I want to go to the library.
   B .... ?
   A .... it has some great history books.

★ **2** Match the questions and statements (1–4) to the responses (a–d).

1 I don't want to go to college.   c
2 Why don't you want to go to the zoo?
3 I hated the dungeon.
4 Why do you want to visit the castle?

a Because it's really cool!
b Because it's boring!
c Why not?
d Why?

★★ **3** Complete the conversation with these phrases.
1.9 Then listen and check.

because	because	because	don't be
why	~~why don't you~~	why not	

Carlos Let's go to the park this afternoon.
Nadia No, thanks.
Carlos Oh, come on, Nadia! ¹*Why don't you* want to go?
Nadia ² .... it's cold.
Carlos Then let's watch a DVD at my house.
Jody Not again, Carlos!
Carlos ³ .... ?
Jody ⁴ .... we always watch DVDs at your house, or my house or Nadia's house. Let's visit the castle.
Zak ⁵ .... ?
Jody Well, ⁶ .... it's fun. And there are dungeons …
Carlos Jody's right. The castle has a great gift shop. I bought some cool things there last year.
Nadia What did you buy?
Carlos A DVD. In the evening, we can watch the DVD.
Nadia Carlos! ⁷ .... silly!

★★ **4** Read the conversation in Exercise 3 again. Are the statements true (T), false (F) or don't know (DK)?

1 Nadia doesn't want to go to the park.   T
2 The friends always watch DVDs at Carlos's house.   ....
3 Jody went to the castle last year.   ....
4 The friends often visit the castle.   ....
5 The gift shop at the castle sells DVDs.   ....
6 Zak wants to watch a DVD in the evening.   ....

★★ **5** Complete the conversation between Tom and Zoe. Use the information in the table and expressions from Exercises 1 and 2.

Friday	go out ✗, stay at home ✓ study for a test on Monday
Saturday	get up early ✓, help mom in the store
Sunday	go to the movies ✗, saw a movie last week

Tom Let's go out on Friday.
Zoe I don't want to go out on Friday.
Tom Why not?
Zoe …

Speaking and Listening page 122

Grammar • Past simple: questions and short answers

★ **1** Match the questions (1–6) to the answers (a–f).

1 Did you visit the castle last week?   c
2 Did Dave see the prisoner in the dungeon?
3 Did the friends watch a historical movie last night?
4 Did Anna enjoy the party?
5 Did the First World War start in 1914?
6 Did you and your friends go home by bus?

a Yes, he did.
b No, we didn't.
c No, I didn't.
d Yes, it did.
e No, she didn't.
f Yes, they did.

★ **2** Complete the questions.

1 Mom left the house early this morning.
  Did Dad leave (Dad / leave) early, too?
2 I read the book.
  .... (she / read) it, too?
3 I wrote the email.
  .... (you / write) the text message, too?
4 I heard a noise outside.
  .... (he / hear) it, too?
5 The fire burned down all the houses.
  .... (it / burn down) the castle, too?
6 He gave her a present.
  .... (they / give) her a present, too?

> **Brain Trainer**
>
> **Writing questions? Remember these four steps:**
>
> | 1 A = Auxiliary | Did |
> | 2 S = Subject | she |
> | 3 I = Infinitive | play tennis |
> | 4 T = Time | yesterday? |
>
> **Now do Exercise 3.**

★★ **3** Complete the conversation.

Sophie   Hi, Thomas. ¹*Did you visit the castle today?* (you / visit / the castle / today?)
Thomas   Yes, I ² .... I went with Amy. She loves old buildings.
Sophie   ³ .... (you / see / the dungeons?)
Thomas   Yes, we ⁴ ....
Sophie   ⁵ .... (Amy / like / them?)
Thomas   No, she ⁶ .... There were spiders, and she's scared of spiders.
Sophie   ⁷ .... (you and Amy / see / rats in the dungeons?)
Thomas   No, we ⁸ .... The dungeons don't have rats!

★★ **4** Write the questions for the answers.

1 A *When did Julia and Brian get married?*
  B Julia and Brian got married three years ago.
2 A .... ?
  B The fire started in the kitchen.
3 A .... ?
  B She wrote a wonderful book about King Arthur.
4 A .... ?
  B My brother graduated from college last year.
5 A .... ?
  B We met Alison in the park.
6 A .... ?
  B I went to the museum because I wanted to see the swords.

Grammar Reference pages 112–113

Reading

1 Read the page from the book quickly. Find:

1 six dates   *1485,* ....
2 two countries   ....
3 six languages   ....
....
4 two English names for boys
....
5 two sports   ....

From Princess of Spain to Queen of England

Catherine of Aragon was born near Madrid in Spain in 1485. Her parents were King Ferdinand and Queen Isabella. Catherine was beautiful, and she was also very smart. She spoke and wrote in Latin and Spanish, and she also spoke English, Flemish, French and Greek. She studied many subjects, including mathematics and philosophy, and she enjoyed dancing, music, archery and horseback riding.

In 1501, Catherine married Prince Arthur of England, but Arthur died five months later. It was a difficult time for Catherine. Then, in 1509, Catherine married Arthur's brother, Henry. She was twenty-three and Henry was seventeen. Two weeks after their wedding, Henry and Catherine became king and queen of England.

At first they were happy, and the English people loved Catherine. But Henry wanted a son, and unfortunately he and Catherine had only one daughter, Mary. In 1525, Henry fell in love with Anne Boleyn and wanted to get married again. He divorced Catherine and, in 1533, he married Anne Boleyn.

Catherine left the castle. Her life was sad and lonely. On January 7, 1536, she died at Kimbolton Castle. Her daughter Mary became queen of England when Henry died.

⁑ 2 ⁑

2 Read the page again. Put the information in the correct order.

a Catherine and Henry got married.   ....
b Catherine and Henry became king and queen of England.   ....
c Catherine was born near Madrid.   .1.
d Anne Boleyn and Henry got married.   ....
e Henry divorced Catherine.   ....
f Catherine's husband, Arthur, died.   ....
g Catherine and Henry's daughter was born.   ....

3 Match the sentence beginnings (1–7) to the endings (a–g).

1 Catherine's parents were   *d*
2 Catherine enjoyed
3 Arthur was
4 In 1509, Catherine and Henry
5 Catherine and Henry's daughter
6 Henry fell in love with
7 Mary became queen of England

a got married.
b Anne Boleyn.
c was Mary.
d King Ferdinand and Queen Isabella.
e when her father died.
f Henry's brother.
g dancing and music.

Listening

1
1.10
Listen to Kate and Nick talking about a movie. Mark the things they mention.

castle ☐   clothes ☐
food ☐   money ☐
rats ☐   shoes ☐

2
1.10
Listen again. Choose the correct options.

1 Nick *loved / didn't mind* the movie *Marie Antoinette*.
2 Kate wants to watch it because she likes the *clothes / music* in the movie.
3 Marie Antoinette *was / wasn't* French.
4 She got married when she was *fifteen / nineteen*.
5 She became queen of France when she was *fifteen / nineteen*.
6 Kate learned about Marie Antoinette from a *documentary / book*.

Writing • A biography

1 **Read the text. In what order is the information in a biography?**

1 Other information .....

2 Work .....

3 Name, place and date of birth *A*

4 Education .....

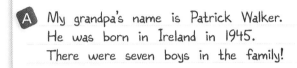

Patrick Walker

A My grandpa's name is Patrick Walker. He was born in Ireland in 1945. There were seven boys in the family!

B My grandpa didn't like school, and he didn't want to go to college. He left school when he was sixteen.

C He found a job in a shoe store. He also worked in a movie theater on weekends. He didn't mind because he loved watching the movies.

D In 1963, Grandpa moved from Ireland to New York. It was exciting because there were a lot of things to do there. Grandpa loved listening to music in cafés. One day a beautiful woman named Rita sang in the café, and Grandpa fell in love with her. In 1965, they got married, and they had one son—my dad!

2 **Complete the table with the information about Patrick Walker.**

Name	¹ *Patrick Walker*
Place of birth	² ....
Date of birth	³ ....
Education	⁴ ....
Work	⁵ .... ⁶ ....
Other information	⁷ .... ⁸ .... ⁹ .... ¹⁰ ....

3 **Read the biography again. Answer the questions.**

1 Where and when was Patrick born?
   He was born in Ireland in 1945.

2 How many brothers did he have?
   ....

3 Did he go to college?
   ....

4 When did he leave school?
   ....

5 What job did he find?
   ....

6 What did he do on weekends?
   ....

7 Did he mind working weekends?
   ....

8 What happened in 1963?
   ....

9 Who did he meet in a café in New York?
   ....

10 When did he get married?
   ....

4 **Think of a person in your family. Write information about him/her in the table.**

Name	....
Place of birth	....
Date of birth	....
Education	....
Work	....
Other information	....

5 **Write a biography about a person in your family. Use the paragraph guide from Exercise 1 and your notes from Exercise 4 to help you.**

....

....

....

....

....

Check 1

Grammar

1 Choose the correct options.

New Message

Send

Hi Emilie,
I ⁰ *'m writing* this email to you from a great hotel.
Mom and I are in New York! We ¹.... here every
summer because Mom's an actress. She doesn't
².... in movies. She ³.... ⁴.... in the theater. At
the moment, she ⁵.... the lines of a new play.
She often ⁶.... me to help her. I ⁷.... mind ⁸.... it
because I ⁹.... to be an actress one day, too.
What about you? What ¹⁰.... to be?
Love,
Jacqueline

0	**a** write	**b** writes	**c** 'm writing
1	**a** come	**b** coming	**c** comes
2	**a** act	**b** acts	**c** acting
3	**a** love	**b** loves	**c** loving
4	**a** work	**b** works	**c** working
5	**a** learning	**b** 's learning	**c** learns
6	**a** is asking	**b** asking	**c** asks
7	**a** 'm not	**b** not	**c** don't
8	**a** do	**b** doing	**c** does
9	**a** want	**b** wanting	**c** wants
10	**a** you want	**b** do you want	**c** does you want

/ 10 points

2 Complete the sentences with the Past simple form of the verbs.

0 Emily's friends went to the castle yesterday, but Emily *didn't go* (not go).

1 Andrea and Max .... (not be) at my house last night.

2 .... (you / stop) at the café after school?

3 They .... (leave) the party at 11 p.m.

4 She .... (carry) her laptop to school in her bag.

5 I .... (see) a great movie on TV last night.

6 .... (your mom / make) breakfast for you this morning?

7 We .... (have) an interesting history lesson yesterday.

8 Harry .... (not do) all his homework last night.

9 The young athlete .... (take) part in the Olympic Games.

10 When .... (the king of France / die)?

/ 10 points

Vocabulary

3 Choose the correct options.

0 Did you watch the documentary / western / fantasy about dolphins on TV? It was interesting, and I learned a lot.

1 I didn't like the action movie. I thought it was expensive / terrible / tasty.

2 Romeo and Juliet got / fell / went in love and wanted to get married.

3 I went ice skating with my friends at the ice skating belt / court / rink.

4 The boys aren't here. They're playing soccer on the soccer court / field / pool.

5 When did he move / graduate / retire to the city?

6 We practice every day at the swimming / basketball / archery court.

7 I didn't understand the science fiction movie. The story was romantic / sad / weird.

8 The famous artist lived in the fifteenth century / plague / war.

9 The queen / knight / servant worked in the kitchen of the castle.

10 What did the student do when he retired / graduated / left from college?

/ 10 points

Speaking

4 Complete the conversation with these words.

about	because	boring	favorite
~~go~~	great	idea	in
thanks	that's	why	

Jane Let's ⁰ go to the movies tonight.

Rob ¹....................... a good idea. There's a fantastic war movie playing.

Will I'm ²....................... . I love war movies. They're my ³....................... type of movie.

Lucy No, ⁴....................... . I don't want to go to the movies.

Jane ⁵....................... don't you want to go?

Lucy ⁶....................... I think war movies are ⁷....................... .

Rob Well, what ⁸....................... a horror movie?

Will That's a good ⁹....................... . I have a great DVD about ghosts.

Jane ¹⁰....................... !

/ 10 points

Translation

5 Translate the sentences.

1 I enjoy going swimming in the summer.

2 We don't usually play basketball on this basketball court.

3 My brother is annoying.

4 The prisoner is in the dungeon.

5 The plague killed thousands of people.

/ 5 points

Dictation

6 Listen and write.
1.11

/ 5 points

Is it a Crime?

Vocabulary • Breaking the rules

★ **1** Look at the pictures. Complete the labels.

bully	~~cheat~~	drop	fight
lie	play	spray	steal

cheat on an exam

.... over a T-shirt

.... to
your parents

.... a younger
student

.... graffiti

.... a purse

.... trash

.... loud music

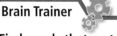
Brain Trainer

Find words that go together:
drop *trash*   spray *graffiti*
Now do Exercise 2.

★ **2** Match 1–6 to a–f to make phrases.

1 copy	a graffiti
2 spray	b trash
3 drop	c school
4 use	d a friend's homework
5 skip	e rude
6 be	f a cell phone in class

★★ **3** Complete the sentences with verbs from Exercise 1.

1 She *lies* to her parents, but they never believe her.
2 I can't hear you. Why do you .... loud music all the time?
3 The boys .... at school when they are angry.
4 I never .... trash because it is bad for the environment.
5 Melissa and her friends .... graffiti in the park. They think it's exciting.
6 The older students sometimes .... the younger ones and take their money and food.

★★ **4** Complete the text with these words.

bully	copy	exams	fight
~~rude~~	school	use	

The students in Mrs. Braddock's class are never ¹ *rude*. They always say "please" and "thank you." They always come to class and never skip ² .... The boys don't ³ .... , and the bigger students don't ⁴ .... the smaller ones and take their money. They never ⁵ .... their cell phones in class, and they never, ever cheat on ⁶ .... or ⁷ .... their friend's homework. They're scared of Mrs. Braddock!

Workbook page 119

Reading

★ **1** Read the story summary quickly. Choose the correct options.

1 Kevin Smith's students *broke / didn't break* the school rules.

2 There was a dance competition *at school / on TV.*

★ **2** Read the story summary again. Match the sentence beginnings (1–5) to the endings (a–e).

1 When Kevin met his new students,   c
2 On Kevin's first day at Morton High School,
3 The students liked
4 The dance classes
5 On the day of the competition,

a the students were excited.
b were fun for the students.
c they were breaking the rules.
d he was angry.
e music and sports.

★★ **3** What school rules were students breaking on Kevin's first day at school?

1 *Max was doing his homework in class.*
2 *Nicola* ....
3 ....
4 ....
5 ....

★★★ **4** Answer the questions.

1 What was Kevin's job?
He was a music teacher.

2 What did he think of Amy's graffiti?
....

3 Where were Derek and Miles?
....

4 What was Carla doing?
....

5 How did Kevin get his idea about the dance classes?
....

6 How did the students feel about the dance classes?
....

Story summary: **From Good to Bad?**

It was the first day at Morton High School for music teacher Kevin Smith, but when he met his students, he wasn't happy. Max was doing his English homework in class and Nicola was copying it. And Amy was spraying graffiti on the wall! Yes, it was a good picture and the colors were beautiful, but she was still breaking the rules. Derek and Miles were fighting at the back of the classroom, Carla was eating candy and dropping her trash on the floor. Kevin was angry. He had a very difficult job to do.

One day, Kevin was on the school soccer field. The students were talking and he was listening to them. Kevin learned something important about these young people—they liked sports and they loved music. Suddenly, he had an idea. Every year there was a dance competition on TV, and Kevin wanted his students to enter the competition. He started dance classes and the students came to them. At first the classes were difficult for the students. But the students enjoyed the classes—and they also started to enjoy their other classes. They didn't break the rules, they listened to their teachers and they passed their exams.

The day of the dance competition came. The students were excited. They were on TV and their friends were watching them! Did they win the competition? Buy the book and find out!

Grammar • Past continuous

★ **(1)** **Look at the picture. Put the words in order to make sentences.**

1 sitting / Two young women / were / in the police station
Two young women were sitting in the police station.
2 wasn't / The police officer / talking / to them
....
3 the two young women / doing / were / What / ?
....
4 and his dog / weren't / The old man / sitting / on chairs
....
5 leaving / was / the police station / An old woman
....
6 wasn't / a drink / The boy / stealing
....
7 Was / wearing / a soccer shirt / the boy / ?
....

★ **(2)** **Complete the questions using the Past continuous. Then look at the picture and answer them.**

1 A *Were* the two young women sitting on chairs?
  B *Yes, they were.*
2 A .... the police officer talking to them?
  B ....
3 A .... the old man and his dog eating?
  B ....
4 A .... the boy wearing soccer cleats?
  B ....
5 A .... the little girl sleeping?
  B ....
6 A .... the man and the woman talking to the police officer?
  B ....
   ....

★★ **(3)** **Complete the sentences with the Past continuous form of the verbs.**

1 The police officer *was standing* (stand) behind a desk.
2 There was a man in front of the desk, but he .... (not talk) to the police officer.
3 "What .... the little girl .... (do)?" "She .... (steal) a watch."
4 The two young women .... (listen) to music.
5 The old man and his dog .... (sleep).
6 The old woman .... (not carry) a box. She .... (carry) a big bag.
7 What .... the man and the woman .... (fight) about?

★★ **(4)** **What were you and your family doing at eight o'clock last night? You can use these ideas or your own ideas. Write five sentences.**

cook dinner	do homework
read the newspaper	talk to a friend
watch TV	write emails

Grammar Reference pages 114–115

Vocabulary • Prepositions of movement

★ 1 Look at the pictures. Complete the crossword.

Crossword:
¹T H R ²O U G H

Across

Down

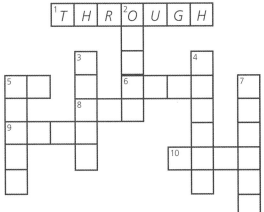

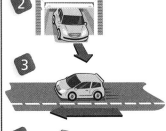

★ 2 Choose the correct options.

1 Walk *across* / *out of* the street to the other side.
2 We walked *through* / *along* the beach.
3 Dora went *out of* / *into* her bedroom and sat on her bed.
4 The mouse ran *under* / *through* the table.
5 The teacher was walking *over* / *around* the classroom.
6 Dad came *out of* / *down* the house.
7 The airplane flew *over* / *off* the town.
8 Come *up* / *down* from that tree! It's time for dinner!

★★ 3 Complete the text with these words.

| along   into   off   out of   over   ~~through~~   up |

1 Martin looked *through* the window.
2 Sarah climbed .... a mountain. It was very tiring.
3 The mouse walked .... the wall.
4 Harry jumped .... the bridge .... the water.
5 Sophie walked .... the bridge.
6 I took the present .... the box.

★★ 4 Complete the text with these words.

| across   along   down   into   into   through   ~~up~~ |

Will Adams climbed ¹ *up* the ladder. Then he climbed ² .... the bedroom ³ .... an open window. A police officer was walking ⁴ .... the street. She saw Will and ran ⁵ .... the street to the house. Just then, Will came ⁶ .... the ladder. "Good evening, Officer," he said. "My key was in the bedroom. Now I have it and I can go ⁷ .... the house and make some coffee. Would you like a cup?"

Workbook page 119

Chatroom Showing interest

Brain Trainer

Do you want to show surprise? Say: *Really?*

Good news? Say: *That's great!* or *That's amazing!*

Bad news? Say: *Oh no!* or *Poor thing!*

Now do Exercise 1.

Speaking and Listening

★ **1** Choose the correct options. Then listen and check.

1.12 1 **A** Mom burned her hand while she was cooking.
   B *That's amazing! /* ~~*Oh no!*~~
2 **A** I won $10,000 in a contest last year!
   B *That's great! / Finally!*
3 **A** I saw the president of the United States yesterday!
   B *Really? / Oh no!* Where did you see him?
4 **A** Finally! You're late! What happened?
   B *Poor thing! / You'll never guess!*
5 **A** I lost my bag on the bus yesterday.
   B *That's great! / Poor thing!*

★ **2** Put the conversation in the correct order.

a Well, what happened? ....
b Really? ....
c I saw Sean Paul in town a few minutes ago. ....
d Finally! Where were you? *1*
e That's amazing! ....
f Yes, he was shopping and I spoke to him. ....
g You'll never guess! ....

Speaking and Listening page 123

102 **Unit 4 • Is it a Crime?**

★★ **3** Complete the conversation with these phrases.
1.13 Then listen and check.

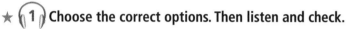

~~finally~~ guess happened poor really that's

Nadia Jody! ¹*Finally!* Why are you late?
Jody Sorry. I missed the bus and walked here.
Nadia Oh no! ² .... thing! What happened?
Jody You'll never ³ .... ! I saw Alicia Keys downtown!
Nadia ⁴ .... ? I don't believe you!
Jody It's true! There was a man behind her and he was stealing money from her bag.
Nadia What did you do?
Jody I shouted and he ran away.
Nadia Then what ⁵ .... ?
Jody Alicia heard me. She thanked me and gave me two tickets to her concert on Saturday.
Nadia ⁶ .... amazing! What are you going to do with them?
Jody I'm going to go to the concert—with you!
Nadia Thanks, Jody! You're a great friend!

★★ **4** Read the conversation in Exercise 3 again. Answer the questions.

1 Why was Jody late?
   She was late because she missed the bus.
2 Where did she see Alicia Keys?
   ....
3 How did Nadia feel when Jody told her about Alicia?
   ....
4 What was the man doing?
   ....
5 How did Alicia thank Jody?
   ....
6 When is Alicia's concert?
   ....

★★ **5** Imagine one of your friends has good news and another friend has bad news. Write two conversations and show interest. You can use your own ideas or the ideas below.

| Friend 1 | win a prize / meet a famous athlete |
| Friend 2 | lose money / break computer |

Grammar • Past simple and Past continuous

Grammar Reference pages 114–115

★ **1** **Read the sentences. Write PS (Past simple) or PC (Past continuous).**

1 They were watching TV. .PC.
2 Julia saw us. ....
3 We were sitting in the café. ....
4 She was writing an email. ....
5 The phone rang. ....
6 They heard a noise. ....

★ **2** **Use two sentences from Exercise 1 to make a sentence with *when*. Then rewrite the sentence with *while*.**

1 (1+6) They were watching TV when they heard a noise.
2 (1+6) While they were watching TV, they heard a noise.
3 ....
4 ....
5 ....
6 ....

★★ **3** **Choose the correct options.**

1 While we *walked* / *were walking* home, it *started* / *was starting* to rain.
2 I *took* / *was taking* a shower when the lights *went out* / *were going out*.
3 When Mom *came* / *was coming* home, Dad *made* / *was making* dinner in the kitchen.
4 Mrs. Ross *slept* / *was sleeping* when the thieves *climbed* / *were climbing* through the living room window.
5 I *found* / *was finding* this interesting website while I *looked* / *was looking* for information on the Internet.
6 The teacher *came* / *was coming* into the classroom while the students *wrote* / *were writing* on the board.

★★ **4** **Complete the sentences with the Past simple and Past continuous forms of the verbs.**

1 While the thief *was climbing* (climb) up the ladder, the police .... (arrive).

2 When the teacher .... (walk) into the classroom, the boys .... (fight).

3 .... you .... (play) loud music when I .... (call) you?

4 While Sam .... (ride) his bike in the park, he .... (lose) his cell phone.

★★ **5** **Write sentences with the Past simple and Past continuous forms of the verbs.**

1 while / Sam / run / he / drop / his money
While Sam was running, he dropped his money.
2 when / we / see / the thief / he / climb / through the window
....
3 they / travel / around the world / when / they / lose / their bags
....
4 my little brother / run / into the kitchen / while / I / make / dinner
....
5 Susie / watch / movie / when / heard / noise
....
6 what / you / do / when / I / call?
....

Reading

1 **Read the email quickly. What is the email about?**

a Maria's birthday presents
b Maria and her friends
c Maria, the bicycle thief and a smart phone

New Message ⊗

Hi Luke,   **Send**

Thank you for remembering my birthday yesterday. Yes, I got some great presents: Mom and Dad gave me a BMX bike, and Grandma gave me a smart phone! And yes, I had a great day. In fact, it was very exciting. Let me tell you about it.

In the morning I went to the park on my BMX. There I met Emily and Roger, and we played basketball for an hour. Then we sat under a tree to eat our sandwiches. I was showing them my new smart phone when I noticed that my BMX bike was missing! I jumped up and looked around the park. And then I saw it! A boy with a black jacket was stealing my bike. "Stop!" I shouted, but the boy got on the bike and rode over the bridge. Then I remembered my smart phone, so I took a photo of him and called the police.

When the police officer arrived, we showed him the photo of the boy. "Come with me to the police station," he said. We were following the police officer over the bridge when we heard a noise. We looked over the side and what do you think we saw? It was the boy in the photo! He was sitting on the grass. "Please help me," he said. "I fell off the bike and I broke my leg."

Well, I got my bike back. It was lucky I had my new smart phone with me.

See you soon!
Maria

---

2 **Read the email again. Answer the questions.**

1 Who gave Maria a smart phone?
   Her grandmother gave her a smart phone.
2 Where did Maria meet her friends?
   ....
3 When did Maria notice her bike was missing?
   ....
4 What was the thief wearing?
   ....
5 What did the thief do when Maria shouted?
   ....
6 What happened to the thief?
   ....

3 **Choose the correct options.**

1 Luke asked Maria about her *bike /* *birthday.*
2 Maria met her friends at the *park / gym.*
3 The friends *were / weren't* playing basketball when a boy stole Maria's bike.
4 The thief *was / wasn't* riding the bike when Maria saw him.
5 Maria took a photo of *the thief / her friends.*
6 The thief was on *the bridge / the grass* when the police officer saw him.

Listening

1 **Listen to four conversations. Match the conversations 1–4 to the pictures a–d.**
1.14

2 **Listen again. Match the sentence beginnings (1–6) to the endings (a–f).**
1.14

1 Anna   a didn't listen to his brother.
2 Max   b was cheating.
3 Eva   c had her name in the book.
4 Sam   d was littering.
5 Lisa   e was stealing.
6 Dave   f thought the music was loud.

Writing • A short story

1 Read the short text. Find four sequencing words.

Last Saturday I went out with my friends. First, we played soccer. Next, we had ice cream. Then we went swimming. Finally, we went to the movies.

1 *First*   3 ....
2 ....   4 ....

2 Read the story. Put the pictures (a–d) in the correct order.

It was nine o'clock in the morning when Sam and his friends arrived at school. There was a lot of litter in the schoolyard, and it was ugly and dirty.

First, they put the litter in the trash can. Next, they looked at the walls of the school. Then they sprayed graffiti on the walls. The graffiti was fantastic! Finally, they washed their hands and had some sandwiches.

A man was walking down the street when he saw Sam and his friends. He was angry, and he shouted at them. But Sam showed the man a poster. It said: "Graffiti Competition this Saturday." "It's OK," said Sam. "We weren't breaking the rules! We were making the school beautiful."

3 Read the story again. Answer the questions.

1 What time was it when Sam and his friends arrived at the school?
It was nine o'clock in the morning.
2 What did the friends do with the litter?
....
3 What did they do to the walls of the school?
....
4 Why was the man angry?
....
5 What did Sam show the man?
....

4 Write a story. Use the words and pictures to help you.

last weekend / sunny / snowboarding
first: go up the mountain
next: snowboard down the mountain
then: go to a café / have a hot chocolate / a man steal their snowboards / stand up to leave / snowboards were missing
finally: call police / police arrive with snowboards / say: "It was easy / find thief. We just / follow / across the snow."

Last weekend it was sunny. Naomi and Liam went snowboarding …

Check ②

Grammar

1 Complete the text with the Past simple or Past continuous form of the verbs.

Last summer I ⁰ *was walking* (walk) in the mountains in Scotland when I ¹........................ (see) a beautiful old castle. I ²........................ (take) photos of it when an old lady ³........................ (stop) her car near me and ⁴........................ (say) good morning. She was very nice and we ⁵........................ (talk) together for a few minutes. That evening, while I ⁶........................ (watch) TV, I ⁷........................ (see) the old lady's face on TV. She was the queen of England!

/ 7 points

2 Complete the text with the comparative or the superlative form of the adjectives.

This year Laura is studying French in Paris, ⁰ *the most romantic* (romantic) city in the world. She is living in a small house. It is ¹........................ (small) than Laura's house in the US, but she loves it there. All the students in Laura's class speak good French, but Laura speaks ²........................ (good) French than the others, and people sometimes think she is French!

Tonight, Laura and two of her friends, Sandrine and Stephanie, are having dinner in a restaurant. The food here is ³........................ (expensive) than café food, but Laura thinks it is ⁴........................ (tasty) food in the world. She also thinks the ice cream here is ⁵........................ (good) in the city! After dinner the girls are meeting their new friends, Henri and Luc. "Henri is two years ⁶........................ (young) than us, but he's very nice," says Laura, "and Luc's jokes are ⁷........................ (bad) in the world, but he makes us laugh."

/ 7 points

3 Complete the sentences with these words.

am	isn't	must	mustn't
should	should	~~to~~	

0 Are you going *to* visit your grandmother this summer?
1 "I don't understand this exercise." "You .... ask your teacher to help you."
2 I .... going to study for my math exam tonight.
3 Dad .... going to buy that car because it's very expensive.
4 You .... eat in the classroom! It's a school rule.
5 "........................ I tell my parents about my problem?" "Yes, that's a good idea."
6 You can't talk in the library. You .... be quiet.

/ 6 points

Vocabulary

4 **Choose the correct options.**

0 Everyone likes Sandra because she's friendly and ... .
  a lazy   **b** selfish   **c** generous

1 When the teacher walked ... the classroom, it was very noisy.
  a into   **b** off   **c** over

2 Alan doesn't like talking to people at parties. He's very ... .
  a smart   **b** shy   **c** cheerful

3 The brothers were ... when their dad came home.
  a fighting   **b** bullying   **c** dropping

4 Paula has brown eyes and long ... hair.
  a thin   **b** big   **c** curly

5 Don't ... metal cans or plastic bottles away. They're dangerous for animals and birds.
  a recycle   **b** protect   **c** throw

6 The friends walked ... the river and talked.
  a on   **b** along   **c** under

7 Jack was ... graffiti on the wall because he was bored.
  a copying   **b** cheating   **c** spraying

8 Ellen wasn't happy when her brother ... to their parents.
  a lied   **b** copied   **c** stole

9 I looked ... the classroom, but I didn't see my backpack.
  a through   **b** around   **c** off

10 It's a good idea to buy ... jars and bottles because you can reuse them.
  a wooden   **b** glass   **c** paper

/ 10 points

Speaking

5 **Complete the conversation with one word in each blank.**

A Good morning. ⁰ *Can* I help you?
B ¹........................ you have the new Justin Bieber CD?
A Yes, we do. ²........................ you go.
B How much ³........................ it?

A It ⁴........................ $16.
B Oh, that's cheap! I'll ⁵........................ it, thanks.

/ 5 points

6 **Match the statements and questions (0–5) to the responses (a–f).**

0 *Avatar* is a great film!   *f*
1 Do you think I look like my sister?
2 I came in first in the competition!
3 I lost my money on the bus this morning.
4 I think Beyoncé is a fantastic singer.
5 The capital of New York State isn't New York. It's Albany.

a Oh no! Poor thing!
b Yes, but she has longer hair and green eyes.
c I think so, too. I love her songs!
d That's great!
e That's right, and the capital of California is Sacramento.
f I disagree. I think it's silly.

/ 5 points

Translation

7 **Translate the sentences.**

1 She was copying her friend's homework when the teacher saw her.
2 He ran across the street.
3 Bob is tall and thin and he has a beard.
4 We must recycle paper and protect the environment.
5 I bought the most expensive watch in the store.

/ 5 points

Dictation

8 **Listen and write.**
1.21

/ 5 points

Grammar Reference

• Present simple

Affirmative		
I/You/We/They	play	basketball.
He/She/It	plays	

Negative		
I/You/We/They	don't (do not) play	basketball.
He/She/It	doesn't (does not) play	

Questions and short answers	
Do I/you/we/they play basketball?	Yes, I/you/we/they do. No, I/you/we/they don't.
Does he/she/it play basketball?	Yes, he/she/it does. No, he/she/it doesn't.

Wh questions
What sports do you play?

Use

We use the Present simple to talk about:
* routines and habits.   *He **practices** every day.*
* things that are true in general.   *They **live** in Rome.*

Form

* To form the third person singular (with *he, she* and *it*), we add *-s, -es* or *-ies* to the verb.
  *She **goes** to the gym.*
* To form the negative, we use *don't (do not)* with *I, you, we* and *they*. We use *doesn't (does not)* with *he, she* and *it*.
  *We **don't play** tennis.*
* To form questions, we use *do* with *I, you, we* and *they*. We use *does* with *he, she* and *it*.
  ***Does** she **like** sports?*

Spelling rules: verb + -s

most verbs: add *-s*
read → reads   play → plays

verbs that end in *-ss, -ch, -sh, -x* and *-o*: add *-es*
kiss → kisses   watch → watches wash → washes   fix → fixes   go → goes

verbs that end in a consonant + *y*: drop the *y* and add *-ies*
try → tries   study → studies

• Verb + -ing

Affirmative		
I/You/We/They	like watching	cartoons.
He/She/It	likes watching	

Negative		
I/You/We/They	don't like watching	cartoons.
He/She/It	doesn't like watching	

Questions
Do I/you/we/they like watching cartoons?
Does he/she/it like watching cartoons?

Use

We use *enjoy, hate, like, love* and *don't mind* + verb + -ing to talk about things we like or don't like doing.
*They **enjoy talking** to their friends on the phone.*

Form

The verbs *enjoy, hate, like, love* and *don't mind* are followed by a verb ending in *-ing*.
*I **don't mind watching** football on TV.*

Spelling rules: verb + -ing

most verbs: add *-ing*   play → playing

verbs that end in *-e*: drop the *-e* and add *-ing* come → coming

verbs that end in one vowel + one consonant: double the consonant and add *-ing*   sit → sitting

• Adverbs of frequency

0%		100%
never/hardly ever	sometimes/often	usually/always

Use

* We often use adverbs of frequency to say how often we do something.
  *I **always** watch the Olympic Games on TV.*
* Adverbs of frequency usually go:
  – before the main verb.
  *I **never** eat pizza.*
  – after the verb *to be*.
  *There is **often** a football game on Monday.*

Grammar practice • Present simple

1 Choose the correct options.

1 My brother *doesn't wear* sneakers to school.
   a don't wear   (b) doesn't wear   c not wear
2 We .... sports after school on Mondays
   and Fridays.
   a do   b does   c doesn't do
3 .... you play the guitar?
   a Do   b Does   c Doesn't
4 Jenny .... swimming every day.
   a go   b goes   c don't go
5 .... Sam do sports on the weekend?
   a Is   b Do   c Does
6 My friends .... play team sports.
   a not   b don't   c doesn't

**2 Complete the questions. Then match the
questions (1–6) to the answers (a–f).**

1 ...*Do*.... you like track, Jack?   e
2 .... Emma like museums?
3 .... they go swimming every day?
4 .... he go snowboarding every winter?
5 .... you play basketball every week, guys?
6 .... it rain every day in Oregon?

a No, they don't.
b No, it doesn't.
c Yes, he does.
d No, she doesn't.
e Yes, I do.
f Yes, we do.

**3 Make sentences or questions with the
Present simple.**

1 she / play / ice hockey / after school ✘
   She doesn't play ice hockey after school.
2 what sports / you / like ?
   ....
3 Max / like / football and basketball ✔
   ....
4 we / do / track / at school ✘
   ....
5 Anna and Daniel / run / every day ?
   ....
6 Jack / go / swimming / every Saturday ✔
   ....

Verb + -ing

**4 Complete the sentences with the correct
form of the verbs.**

love: ☺☺	like/enjoy: ☺	don't mind: 😐
don't like: ☹	hate: ☹☹	

1 I ☺☺ *love watching* (watch) movies at the
   movie theater.
2 John ☹ .... (do) sports
   at school.
3 The dog ☺ .... (play) in the
   yard with the ball.
4 The girls 😐 .... (watch) sports
   on TV.
5 She ☹☹ .... (wear) sneakers.
6 Lucy and Ben ☺☺ .... (go)
   skateboarding on the weekend.

Adverbs of frequency

**5 Put the adverbs of frequency in the
correct order.**

~~always~~	hardly ever	never
often	sometimes	usually

1 .... / 0%
2 .... / ....
3 .... / *always*   100%

6 Put the words in the correct order.

1 T-shirts / I / wear / never / to school
   I never wear T-shirts to school.
2 the gym / She / goes / often / to
   ....
3 makes / pizza / hardly ever / My mother
   ....
4 a party / is / on the weekend / usually / There
   ....
5 his homework / Sam / on a laptop / always /
   does
   ....
6 sometimes / on TV / There / a good movie / is
   ....

Grammar Reference

• Present continuous

Affirmative		
I	'm (am) watching	
You/We/They	're (are) watching	a cartoon.
He/She/It	's (is) watching	
Negative		
I	'm not (am not) watching	
You/We/They	aren't (are not) watching	a cartoon.
He/She/It	isn't (is not) watching	
Questions and short answers		
Am I watching a cartoon?	Yes, I am. No, I'm not.	
Are you/we/they watching a cartoon?	Yes, you/we/they are. No, you/we/they aren't.	
Is he/she/it watching a cartoon?	Yes, he/she/it is. No, he/she/it isn't.	
Wh questions		
What am I watching? What are you/we/they watching? What is he/she/it watching?		

Use

We use the Present continuous to talk about actions that are happening now, at the moment of speaking.
We're having breakfast at the moment.

Form

* We form the Present continuous with *to be* (*am*, *is* or *are*) + main verb + *-ing*.
  They're making pizzas.
* To form the negative, we add *not* after *am*, *is* or *are*.
  It isn't raining at the moment.
* The word order changes in questions: *Am/Is/Are* + subject + main verb + *-ing*.
  Are you doing your homework?
* In short answers, we do not repeat the main verb.
  A *Is she eating popcorn?*   **B** *Yes, she is.*

• Present simple and Present continuous

Present simple	Present continuous
I often play tennis.	I'm playing basketball today.

Use

Present simple

We use the Present simple to talk about:
* routines and habits.
  I go to the movies every weekend.
* things that are true in general.
  We enjoy action movies.

Time expressions

adverbs of frequency (*never, hardly ever, sometimes, often, usually, always*), *every day, every Saturday, on the weekend, after school, on Wednesdays*

Present continuous

We use the Present continuous to talk about things that are happening now, at the moment of speaking.
She's watching her favorite TV show at the moment.

Time expressions

now, right now, today, at the moment

Grammar practice • Present continuous

1 Complete the table.

lose	1 *losing*
2	running
begin	3 ....
4	studying
look	5 ....
smile	6 ....
7	sitting
wait	8 ....

2 Put the words in the correct order.

1 football / not / at the moment / is / He / playing
He is not playing football at the moment.

2 sitting / We / the shopping mall / in / are
....

3 books / The girls / are / reading / their / now
....

4 Is / at the moment / her homework / doing / she / ?
....

5 smiling / not / You / in the photo / are
....

6 I / a gym bag / not / am / carrying
....

3 Complete the conversation with the correct form of the Present continuous.

Nicole Hi, Adam. [1] *Are you doing* (you / do) your homework?

Adam Yes, I am. I [2] .... (try) to finish it because Rafael Nadal [3] .... (play) tennis on TV.

Nicole I know. Dad [4] .... (watch) it.

Adam [5] .... (Nadal / win)?

Nicole I don't think so. Dad [6] .... (not smile).

Adam You [7] .... (joke)!

Nicole No, I [8] .... Dad's angry because Nadal [9] .... (lose).

Adam Oh no! It's a good thing I [10] .... (not watch) it!

• Present simple and Present continuous

4 Read the sentences and write Present simple (PS) or Present continuous (PC).

1 I usually <u>eat</u> *PS* pizza, but I'<u>m eating</u> *PC* pasta today.

2 Jack often <u>does</u> .... judo after school, but he'<u>s studying</u> .... for an exam today.

3 We'<u>re watching</u> .... a comedy at the moment, but we usually <u>watch</u> .... action movies.

4 I sometimes <u>go</u> .... to the beach after school, but I'<u>m helping</u> .... my mom in the store at the moment.

5 Charles and Emma usually <u>study</u> .... after school, but they <u>aren't studying</u> .... today.

6 Amanda <u>is sitting</u> .... with me now, but she usually <u>sits</u> .... with Maria.

5 Complete the sentences with the Present simple or Present continuous form of the verbs.

1 Daniel and Anna usually *do* (do) judo after school, but they *are running* (run) in the park now.

2 Sam .... (play) tennis with Fiona today, but he never .... (win)!

3 We often .... (watch) TV in the evening, but at the moment we .... (study) for our history exam.

4 The film director usually .... (make) science fiction movies, but he .... (work) on a documentary at the moment.

5 Paula .... (wear) her black jeans today, but she .... (usually not wear) them to school.

Grammar Reference

• Past simple: *to be*

To be: affirmative		
I/He/She/It You/We/They	was were	at the castle.

To be: negative		
I/He/She/It You/We/They	wasn't (was not) weren't (were not)	at the castle.

To be: questions and short answers	
Was I/he/she/it at the castle?	Yes, I/he/she/it was. No, I/he/she/it wasn't.
Were you/we/they at the castle?	Yes, you/we/they were. No, you/we/they weren't.

• Past simple: affirmative and negative

Regular verbs: affirmative and negative		
I/You/He/She/ It/We/They	lived	in an old house.
I/You/He/She/ It/We/They	didn't (did not) live	in an old house.

Irregular verbs: affirmative and negative		
I/You/He/She/ It/We/They	went	to New York.
I/You/He/She/ It/We/They	didn't (did not) go	to New York.

Use

We use the Past simple to talk about states or actions that began and finished in the past.
*I **was** at home yesterday afternoon.*
*The war **ended** in 1945.*

Form

• To form the Past simple of regular verbs, we add
  -ed, -d or *-ied* to the verb.
• Irregular verbs have different past forms.

(See the **Irregular Verb List**, page 126.)

• To form the negative of regular and irregular verbs,
  we use *did not (didn't)* + the main verb in the
  infinitive.
  *We **didn't go** to school yesterday.*

• Spelling rules: verb + *-ed*

most verbs: add *-ed* *kill → killed*   *visit → visited*
verbs that end in *-e*: add *-d* *live → lived*   *die → died*
verbs that end in consonant + *y*: drop the *y* and add *-ied* *carry → carried*   *study → studied*
verbs that end in one vowel + one consonant: double the consonant and add *-ed* *drop → dropped*

• Past simple: questions and short answers

Regular verbs: questions and short answers
Did I/you/he/she/it/we/they graduate from college? Yes, I/you/he/she/it/we/they did. No, I/you/he/she/it/we/they didn't (did not).

Irregular verbs: questions and short answers
Did I/you/he/she/it/we/they see a ghost? Yes, I/you/he/she/it/we/they did. No, I/you/he/she/it/we/they didn't (did not).

Wh questions
What did he do?   Where did they go?

Form

• To form questions, we use *did* + the main verb in
  the infinitive. The word order also changes: *did* +
  subject + main verb.
  ***Did** she **leave** home when she was eighteen?*
• In short answers, we do not repeat the main verb.
  A ***Did** you **enjoy** the movie?*   **B** *Yes, I **did**.*

Grammar practice • Past simple: *to be*

1 Choose the correct options.

1 I didn't like the movie because it (was) / wasn't boring.
2 The students had an exam, so they wasn't / weren't happy.
3 Michael Jackson wasn't / weren't British. He was / wasn't from the United States.
4 "Was / Were you tired last night?" "Yes, I was / were."
5 The queen was / were in the castle, but the king wasn't / weren't with her.
6 "Was / Were Megan with her friends?" "No, she wasn't / weren't."

• Past simple: affirmative and negative

2 Are the verbs regular (R) or irregular (I)?

1 Jack <u>left</u> the party with his friend, Emily.   I
2 The boy <u>carried</u> the bike to his house.   ....
3 We <u>stopped</u> at a café downtown..   ....
4 Alice <u>had</u> a good time with her friends.   ....
5 The children <u>saw</u> a ghost in the park.   ....
6 We <u>learned</u> about the kings and queens of England last year.   ....

3 Put the words in the correct order.

1 enjoy / last night / the party / didn't / I
 I didn't enjoy the party last night.
2 left / ago / school / ten / years / My big brother
 ....
3 in / was / born / nineteenth / the / She / century
 ....
4 They / to / month / Argentina / went / last
 ....
5 here / evening / Jake / arrived / yesterday
 ....
6 in / a lot of people / The disease / killed / 1665
 ....

4 Write sentences with the Past simple.

1 John / not have / coffee / with breakfast
 John didn't have coffee with breakfast.
2 we / visit / the museum / last month
 ....
3 Sylvia and Amy / come / to my house / yesterday afternoon
 ....
4 I / not see / the documentary / on TV / last night
 ....
5 we / do / judo / at school / last Monday
 ....
6 the prisoners / not escape / from the dungeon
 ....

• Past simple: questions and short answers

5 Write questions and short answers.

1 Mark / like / his new teacher? ✓
 A *Did Mark like his new teacher?*
 B *Yes, he did.*
2 the girls / go / to the library / yesterday afternoon? ✗
 A ....
 B ....
3 Lauren / take / photos / of the castle? ✓
 A ....
 B ....
4 you / do / your homework / on your laptop? ✗
 A ....
 B ....
5 it / happen / yesterday? ✓
 A ....
 B ....
6 she / visit / the museum? ✗
 A ....
 B ....

Grammar Reference

• Past continuous

Affirmative		
I/He/She/It You/We/They	was talking were talking	in class.
Negative		
I/He/She/It You/We/They	wasn't (was not) talking weren't (were not) talking	in class.
Questions and short answers		
Was I/he/she/it talking in class?	Yes, I/he/she/it was. No, I/he/she/it wasn't.	
Were you/we/they talking in class?	Yes, you/we/they were. No, you/we/they weren't.	
Wh questions		
What were they doing in the library yesterday?		

Time expressions

an hour ago   at eleven o'clock   last week
yesterday   yesterday evening

Use

We use the Past continuous to describe actions in progress at a certain time in the past.
*At midnight last night I **was sleeping**.*

Form

• We form the Past continuous with *was* or *were* + main verb + *-ing*.
*At eight o'clock they **were walking** to school.*

• To form the negative, we add *not* after *was* or *were*.
*It **wasn't raining** at ten o'clock last night.*

• The word order changes in questions: *was/were* + subject + main verb + *-ing*.
***Were** the students **skipping** school yesterday?*

• In short answers, we do not repeat the main verb.
A *Was Anna **cheating** on the exam?*
B *Yes, she **was**.*

• Past simple and Past continuous

when	*while*
We were playing tennis when Maria took our photo.	While we were playing tennis, Maria took our photo.

Use

• We use the Past simple for actions that began and finished in the past.
*We **had** dinner at a great restaurant last night.*

• We use the Past continuous for actions that were in progress at a certain time in the past.
*We **were having** dinner at eight o'clock last night.*

When and *while*

• We can use the Past simple and the Past continuous to describe an action that happened while another longer action was in progress. We use the Past simple for the shorter action and the Past continuous for the longer action. To connect the two actions, we use *when* or *while*.
  – We usually use *when* + Past simple.
    *We were laughing **when** Martin **came** in.*
    ***When** Martin **came** in, we were laughing.*
  – We usually use *while* + Past continuous.
    ***While** she **was running**, she dropped her bag.*
    *She dropped her bag **while** she **was running**.*

• When we start a sentence with *while* or *when*, we use a comma.
*While I **was waiting**, I **read** a book.*

Grammar practice • Past continuous

1 Complete the sentences with the Past continuous form of these verbs.

| do | play | sit | talk | watch | ~~wear~~ |

1 Liam *was wearing* a white T-shirt yesterday.
2 The boys .... judo at the gym at ten.
3 We .... a horror movie last night at eleven o'clock.
4 I .... to my mom when Dad came home.
5 Emma and Laura .... a computer game at four o'clock this afternoon.
6 You .... in the living room when it started to rain.

2 Write sentences with the Past continuous.

1 Max was eating pasta. ✘ (make pasta)
  Max wasn't eating pasta. He was making pasta.
2 Julia and I were watching TV. ✘ (listen to music)
  ....
3 Ben and Daniel were walking. ✘ (run)
  ....
4 I was doing my homework. ✘ (read my emails)
  ....
5 You were walking to school. ✘ (ride your bike)
  ....

3 Put the words in the correct order.

1 last night / was / What / on TV / watching / Emma / at nine o'clock / ?
  What was Emma watching on TV at nine o'clock last night?
2 an exam / Were / this / they / taking / morning / ?
  ....
3 yesterday / Was / playing / soccer / Billy / ?
  ....
4 having / they / at the party / fun / Were / ?
  ....
5 doing / yesterday / were / What / you / morning / at six o'clock / ?
  ....
6 cheating / Was / Anna / on the exam / ?
  ....

4 Complete the questions and answers.

1 A *Was Daniel listening* (Daniel / listen) to the teacher?
  B No, *he wasn't.*
2 A .... (the girls / play) in the park yesterday?
  B Yes, ...
3 A .... (she / do) gymnastics at three o'clock?
  B Yes, ...
4 A .... (they / sit) in the café at five o'clock?
  B No, ...
5 A .... (it / rain) at midnight?
  B Yes, ...
6 A .... (Anna / use) her laptop?
  B No, ...

• Past simple and Past continuous

5 Choose the correct options.

1 We *left* / (*were leaving*) the bank when we (*saw*) / *were seeing* the thief.
2 While we *sat* / *were sitting* in the park, a man *stole* / *was stealing* my bag.
3 When the police *arrived* / *were arriving*, the boys *fought* / *were fighting*.
4 He *played* / *was playing* tennis when the rain *started* / *was starting*.
5 While Edward *didn't look* / *wasn't looking*, Max *copied* / *was copying* his answers.

6 Write sentences with the Past simple and Past continuous.

1 he / watch / a movie / when / his dad / call him
  He was watching a movie when his dad called him.
2 while / they / play / tennis / Jack / arrive
  ....
3 when / I / see / them / they / wear sunglasses
  ....
4 Emma / do / her homework / while / she wait
  ....
5 I sit / in the living room / when / my uncle come in
  ....
6 while / we / walk / to the library / I drop / my keys
  ....

Vocabulary

Play the Game!

Unit vocabulary

1 Translate the words.

Sports

archery ....

basketball ....

football ....

gymnastics ....

horseback riding ....

ice hockey ....

ice skating ....

judo ....

mountain biking ....

skateboarding ....

skiing ....

snowboarding ....

soccer ....

swimming ....

tennis ....

track ....

2 Translate the words.

Compound nouns

basketball court ....

football field ....

hockey stick ....

ice skates ....

ice skating rink ....

judo belt ....

soccer cleats ....

soccer field ....

swimming pool ....

swimsuit ....

tennis court ....

tennis racket ....

Vocabulary extension

3 Match the photos to the words in the box. Use your dictionary if necessary. Write the words in English and in your language.

| diving | ~~golf~~ | rowing | sailing | volleyball |

1 ....*golf*........ ....

2 ....

3 ....

4 ....

5 ....
....

Vocabulary

The Big Picture

Unit vocabulary

1 Translate the words.

Types of movies

action movie ....

animation ....

comedy ....

documentary ....

fantasy ....

historical movie ....

horror movie ....

martial arts movie ....

musical ....

science fiction movie ....

war movie ....

western ....

2 Translate the words.

Adjectives

annoying ....

awesome ....

boring ....

exciting ....

expensive ....

funny ....

romantic ....

sad ....

scary ....

tasty ....

terrible ....

weird ....

Vocabulary extension

3 Match the photos to the words in the box. Use your dictionary if necessary. Write the words in English and in your language.

| aisle | box office | seat | ~~screen~~ | usher |

1 .....*screen*........ .... 2 ....

3 ....

4 .... 5 ....

Vocabulary

Past Lives

Unit vocabulary

1 Translate the words.

History

army ....
castle ....
century ....
die ....
dungeon ....
kill ....
king ....
knight ....
plague ....
prisoner ....
queen ....
servant ....
soldier ....
sword ....
war ....

2 Translate the words and expressions.

Life events

be born ....
die ....
fall in love ....
find a job ....
get married ....
go to college ....
graduate ....
have a baby ....
leave home ....
move ....
retire ....
start school ....

Vocabulary extension

3 Match the pictures to the words in the box. Use your dictionary if necessary. Write the words in English and in your language.

| crown | falconer | monk | peasant | shield |

1 .....*crown*..... ....
2 ....
3 ....
4 ....
5 ....

Vocabulary

Is It a Crime?

Unit vocabulary

1 Translate the words and expressions.

Breaking the rules

be rude ....
bully ....
cheat on an exam ....
copy someone's homework
 ....
fight ....
lie ....
litter ....
play loud music ....
skip school ....
spray graffiti ....
steal something ....
use a cell phone in class
 ....

2 Translate the words.

Prepositions of movement

across ....
along ....
around ....
down ....
into ....
off ....
out of ....
over ....
through ....
under ....
up ....

Vocabulary extension

3 Match the pictures to the words in the box. Use your dictionary if necessary. Write the words in English and in your language.

| arson | burglar | shoplift | smoke | ~~vandalize~~ |

1 *vandalize* ....
2 ....
3 ....
4 ....
5 ....

Speaking and Listening

Opinions

• Speaking

1 Complete the conversations with one word
1.32 in each blank. Then listen and check.

1 **A** What do you *think* of Sebastian Vettel?
  B I .... he's amazing.
2 **A** .... you like tennis?
  B No, I don't. I think ....'s boring.
3 **A** My .... sport is judo.
  B Really? I .... judo, too.

2 Complete the conversation with these words and
1.33 phrases. Then listen and check.

don't	do you	favorite teams	I love
I think	like	~~what do you think~~	

Lily   ¹*What do you think* of swimming, Diana?
Diana   ² .... swimming. What about you, John?
John   ³ .... swimming is boring, and I ⁴ .... like swimming pools. Anyway, I want to watch the football game this afternoon. The Cowboys are playing. The Patriots and the Cowboys are my ⁵ .... ⁶ .... like the Cowboys, Vince?
Vince   Hmm. I don't ⁷ .... them, but the Patriots are great.
Lily   Right. So the boys can watch football, and you and I can swim, Diana.
Diana   Cool!

• Listening

3 Listen to the conversation. Are the statements
1.34 true (T), false (F) or don't know (DK)?

1 Alex likes basketball.   *T*
2 Maria doesn't enjoy basketball.   ....
3 Alex likes horseback riding.   ....
4 Maria enjoys horseback riding.   ....
5 Alex loves archery.   ....

4 Listen again. Answer the questions.
1.34
1 Is there a basketball game between the Spurs and the Mavericks tonight?
  No, there isn't. There's a basketball game between the Spurs and the Heat.
2 Does Maria want to watch the basketball game?
  ....
3 Why does Maria sometimes go to the basketball court?
  ....
4 What is Maria's favorite sport?
  ....
5 What is Alex's favorite sport?
  ....

Speaking and Listening

Suggestions

• Speaking

1 Complete the conversations with one word
1.35 in each blank. Then listen and check.

1 **A** *How* about asking Helen to come with us
to the movies?
B That's a good ....
2 **A** .... don't we visit the Film
Museum this weekend?
B ...., thanks! It's boring.
3 **A** ....'s watch a DVD at my
house tonight.
B I'm .... ! Which DVD do
you have?
4 **A** Why ....n't we watch
the new comedy?
B .... way! I hate comedies!

2 Complete the conversation with these words and
1.36 phrases. Then listen and check.

~~come~~	coming	great	let's meet
no, thanks	that's a	way	

Dave What are you doing, Paul?
Paul I'm getting ready to go out.
Dave Where are you going?
Paul To the museum. Why don't you
¹ *come* with me?
Dave No ² .... ! I hate museums.
Look, how about ³ .... to
the gym with me?
Paul ⁴ .... ! You hate museums,
but I hate sports.
Dave OK. You go to the museum and I'll go
to the gym. But ⁵ .... at
the café later to hang out.
Paul ⁶ .... good idea.
Dave And we can go to the movies in the
evening.
Paul ⁷ .... ! I'm in!

• Listening

3 Listen to the conversation. Choose
1.37 the correct options.

1 Susie and (Marcia)/ Adam want to see
a historical movie.
2 Historical movies *are / aren't* Susie's
favorite movies.
3 Adam *likes / doesn't like* historical movies.
4 Adam *wants / doesn't want* Susie and Marcia
to watch a movie with him.
5 Susie and Marcia *want / don't want* to watch
a movie with Adam.

4 Listen again. Answer the questions.
1.37
1 What is Susie reading?
*She's reading a review of the new
Edward Morris movie.*
2 Why does Susie want to see the historical movie?
....
3 Who does Marcia like?
....
4 What kind of movie does Adam want to see?
....
5 When does Adam want to go to the movies?
....

Speaking and Listening

Reasoning

• Speaking

1 **Put the conversation in the correct order.**
1.38 **Then listen and check.**

a Well, I don't want to see ghosts. ....
b Why? ....
c Why not? ....
d Because I'm scared of ghosts. ....
e Because I love places with ghosts in them. ....
f I want to go to the Tower of London. *1* ....

2 **Complete the conversation with these words**
1.39 **and phrases. Then listen and check.**

because x3	don't be silly	don't you
~~say~~	why	why not

Ann It's beautiful here, Sam! Now I want to
take a photo of us in front of the castle.
¹ *Say* "Cheese"!

Sam No! I don't want you to take my photo.

Ann ² .... ?

Sam ³ .... the sun is in my eyes.

Ann Oh, all right. Well, let's walk over
the bridge.

Sam ⁴ .... ?

Ann ⁵ .... we can see the castle
from there!

Sam I don't want to see the castle.

Zoe Cheer up, Sam. Why ⁶ ....
want to see the castle?

Sam ⁷ .... I'm tired.

Zoe ⁸ ...., Sam. We can take
a good photo there.

Sam Oh, OK.

• Listening

3 **Listen to the conversation.**
1.40 **Choose the correct options.**

1 Barbara is *at home*.
(a) at home **b** at school **c** at the movies
2 Barbara is watching .... .
a a historical movie **b** a documentary
c a movie about wildlife
3 Walter is Barbara's .... .
a father **b** teacher **c** brother

4 **Listen again. Answer the questions.**
1.40
1 What is the TV show about?
The TV show is about the plague
in the fourteenth century.
2 Who doesn't want to watch the show?
....
3 What does Barbara think of the show?
....
4 Why does Walter hate rats?
....
5 When is Walter's history test?
....

Speaking and Listening

Showing interest

• Speaking

1 Choose the correct options. Then listen and check.

1.41

1 **A** I have two tickets for the rock concert on Friday.
   B *That's great!* / *Poor thing!* Do you want to take me with you?

2 **A** I can't come to the park with you. I have a lot of homework.
   B *Oh no!* / *Really?* I don't want to go alone.

3 **A** I saw Rafa Nadal in the street yesterday.
   B *Really?* / *That's amazing!* Lucky you!

4 **A** I think a thief took my cell phone.
   B *Really?* / *Poor thing!* Are you sure you didn't leave it at home?

2 Complete the conversation with these words and phrases. Then listen and check.

1.42

| ~~finally~~ | never | poor | really | that's great |

Josh Hi, Eva! I have something to tell you!

Eva Josh! [1] *Finally*! Why are you late? And what happened to your eye?

Josh I fell.

Eva [2] ....thing! Does your eye hurt?

Josh No, but I broke my sunglasses.

Eva Oh no! How did it happen?

Josh You'll [3] .... guess. I was at the train station when I saw a man taking a wallet from a woman's bag.

Eva [4] .... ? What did you do?

Josh I ran after him, but while I was running, I fell over a small dog.

Eva Did you catch the thief?

Josh No, I didn't. A police officer caught him, but the woman thanked me anyway and gave me $15.

Eva [5] .... !

• Listening

3 Listen to the conversation. Answer the questions.

1.43

1 Who was waiting for Erica?
   Charlie was waiting for her.

2 Who saw Erica at the mall?
   ....

3 Who was angry with Erica?
   ....

4 Whose party can't Erica go to?
   ....

4 Listen again. Are the statements true (T), false (F) or don't know (DK)?

1.43

1 Erica didn't go to her science class today.   *T*

2 She went to her English class today.   ....

3 She was at a café when her teacher saw her.   ....

4 She often skips school.   ....

5 Charlie knows Jim.   ....

Pronunciation

Consonants

Symbol	Example	Your examples
/p/	**p**ark	
/b/	**b**ig	
/t/	**t**oy	
/d/	**d**og	
/k/	**c**ar	
/g/	**g**ood	
/tʃ/	**ch**air	
/dʒ/	**j**eans	
/f/	**f**un	
/v/	**v**isit	
/θ/	**th**ree	
/ð/	**th**ey	
/s/	**s**wim	
/z/	**z**oo	
/ʃ/	**sh**oe	
/ʒ/	televi**s**ion	
/h/	**h**ot	
/m/	**m**ap	
/n/	**n**otes	
/ŋ/	si**ng**	
/l/	**l**aptop	
/r/	**r**oom	
/y/	**y**ellow	
/w/	**w**atch	

Vowels

Symbol	Example	Your examples
/ɪ/	r**i**ch	
/ɛ/	**e**gg	
/æ/	r**a**t	
/ɑ/	b**o**x	
/ʌ/	f**u**n	
/ʊ/	p**u**t	
/i/	**ea**t	
/eɪ/	gr**ay**	
/aɪ/	m**y**	
/ɔɪ/	b**oy**	
/u/	b**oo**t	
/oʊ/	n**o**te	
/aʊ/	n**ow**	
/ɪr/	h**ear**	
/ɛr/	h**air**	
/ɑr/	st**ar**	
/ɔ/	d**o**g	
/ʊr/	t**our**	
/ɔr/	d**oor**	
/ə/	**a**mong	
/ɚ/	sh**ir**t	

Pronunciation practice

Unit 1 • Verb endings: /s/, /z/, /ɪz/

1 Listen and repeat.
1.59

dances	enjoys	hates	loses	loves
practices	runs	takes	writes	

2 Complete the table.

dances	enjoys	hates	loses	loves
practices	runs	takes	writes	

/s/	/z/	/ɪz/
....	....	....
....	....	....
....	....	....

3 Listen and check.
1.60

Unit 2 • Word stress in adjectives

1 Listen and repeat.
1.61

boring	expensive	funny
romantic	scary	terrible

2 Circle the word with the correct stress.

1 boring   boring
2 expensive   expensive
3 funny   funny
4 romantic   romantic
5 scary   scary
6 terrible   terrible

3 Listen and check.
1.62

Unit 3 • Verb endings: /t/, /d/, /ɪd/

1 Listen. Write the correct pronunciation for
1.63 the verbs: /t/, /d/ or /ɪd/.

Last night Jack played .... football and watched .... TV. He started .... his homework at 10 p.m.

2 Complete the table.

carried	loved	started
stopped	visited	watched

/t/	/d/	/ɪd/
....	....	....
....	....	....

3 Listen and check.
1.64

Unit 4 • was and were: strong and weak forms

1 Listen and repeat.
1.65
1 She was at home.
2 Yes, you were.
3 They were doing judo.
4 We weren't happy.
5 What were you doing?
6 No, I wasn't.

2 Listen again. Mark the sentences that stress
1.65 was/wasn't or were/weren't.

1 She was at home.
2 Yes, you were.
3 They were doing judo.
4 We weren't happy.
5 What were you doing?
6 No, I wasn't.

3 Listen and check.
1.66

Irregular Verb List

Verb	Past Simple	Past Participle
be	was/were	been
become	became	become
begin	began	begun
break	broke	broken
bring	brought	brought
build	built	built
buy	bought	bought
can	could	been able
catch	caught	caught
choose	chose	chosen
come	came	come
cost	cost	cost
cut	cut	cut
do	did	done
drink	drank	drunk
drive	drove	driven
eat	ate	eaten
feel	felt	felt
fight	fought	fought
find	found	found
fly	flew	flown
forget	forgot	forgotten
get	got	gotten
give	gave	given
go	went	gone/been
have	had	had
hear	heard	heard
hold	held	held
keep	kept	kept
know	knew	known

Verb	Past Simple	Past Participle
leave	left	left
lose	lost	lost
make	made	made
mean	meant	meant
meet	met	met
pay	paid	paid
put	put	put
read /rɪd/	read /rɛd/	read /rɛd/
run	ran	run
say	said	said
see	saw	seen
sell	sold	sold
send	sent	sent
sing	sang	sung
sit	sat	sat
sleep	slept	slept
speak	spoke	spoken
swim	swam	swum
take	took	taken
teach	taught	taught
tell	told	told
think	thought	thought
throw	threw	thrown
understand	understood	understood
wake	woke	woken
wear	wore	worn
win	won	won
write	wrote	written

My Assessment Profile Starter Unit

1 What can I do? Mark (✓) the options in the table.

⏮ = I need to study this again.   ⏸ = I'm not sure about this.   ▶ = I'm happy with this.   ⏭ = I do this very well.

		⏮	⏸	▶	⏭
Grammar (pages 4 and 5)	• I can use all forms of *to be* in the Present simple. • I can use all forms of *have* in the Present simple. • I can use all forms of *there is/are* in the Present simple. • I can use personal and object pronouns correctly. • I can use the possessive *'s*. • I can use possessive adjectives and pronouns correctly.				
Vocabulary (pages 6 and 7)	• I can talk about places in a town. • I can talk about possessions. • I can talk about countries and nationalities. • I can talk about people.				
Reading (page 8)	• I can read and understand profiles of people on a social network.				
Writing (page 8)	• I can write my own profile for a social network.				
Speaking (page 9)	• I can ask someone for information about people and give information about myself.				
Listening (page 9)	• I can understand a conversation between friends.				

2 What new words and expressions can I remember?

words

....

expressions

....

3 How can I practice other new words and expressions?

record them on my MP3 player ☐   write them in a notebook ☐
practice them with a friend ☐   translate them into my language ☐

4 What English have I learned outside class?

	words	expressions
on the radio		
in songs		
in movies		
on the Internet		
on TV		
with friends		

My Assessment Profile   Unit

1 **What can I do? Mark (✓) the options in the table.**

⏪ = I need to study this again.   ⏸ = I'm not sure about this.   ▶ = I'm happy with this.   ⏩ = I do this very well.

		⏪	⏸	▶	⏩
Vocabulary (pages 10 and 13)	• I can talk about fifteen sports. • I can talk about sports equipment and places where people play sports.				
Reading (pages 11 and 16)	• I can read and understand an article about the Olympic Games and an article about the superstitions of famous athletes.				
Grammar (pages 12, 13 and 15)	• I can use the Present simple to talk about routines and habits and things that are true in general. • I can say what I like and don't like using *enjoy, hate, like, love* and *don't mind* + verb + *-ing*. • I can use adverbs of frequency to say how often something happens.				
Pronunciation (page 12)	• I can pronounce verb endings in the Present simple correctly.				
Speaking (pages 14 and 15)	• I can ask for opinions and give my opinion.				
Listening (page 16)	• I can understand a radio show.				
Writing (page 17)	• I can use punctuation correctly. • I can write a description of a sport.				

2 **What new words and expressions can I remember?**

words

....

expressions

....

3 **How can I practice other new words and expressions?**

record them on my MP3 player   ☐   write them in a notebook   ☐
practice them with a friend   ☐   translate them into my language   ☐

4 **What English have I learned outside class?**

	words	expressions
on the radio		
in songs		
in movies		
on the Internet		
on TV		
with friends		

My Assessment Profile Unit

1 **What can I do? Mark (✓) the options in the table.**

⏪ = I need to study this again.   ⏸ = I'm not sure about this.   ▶ = I'm happy with this.   ⏩ = I do this very well.

		⏪	⏸	▶	⏩
Vocabulary (pages 20 and 23)	• I can talk about twelve different types of movies. • I can use adjectives.				
Reading (pages 21 and 26)	• I can read and understand a blog entry about a film museum and an interview in a magazine with a movie extra.				
Grammar (pages 22 and 25)	• I can use the Present continuous to talk about actions in progress. • I know when to use the Present simple and when to use the Present continuous.				
Pronunciation (page 23)	• I know where the stress is in adjectives.				
Speaking (pages 24 and 25)	• I can make suggestions and respond to them.				
Listening (page 26)	• I can understand an interview in the street.				
Writing (page 27)	• I can use linking words correctly. • I can write a movie review.				

2 **What new words and expressions can I remember?**

words

....

expressions

....

3 **How can I practice other new words and expressions?**

record them on my MP3 player ☐   write them in a notebook ☐

practice them with a friend ☐   translate them into my language ☐

4 **What English have I learned outside class?**

	words	expressions
on the radio		
in songs		
in movies		
on the Internet		
on TV		
with friends		

My Assessment Profile   Unit

1 What can I do? Mark (✓) the options in the table.

⏪ = I need to study this again.   ⏸ = I'm not sure about this.   ▶ = I'm happy with this.   ⏩ = I do this very well.

		⏪	⏸	▶	⏩
Vocabulary (pages 30 and 33)	• I can use fifteen words to talk about history. • I can use twelve words and expressions to talk about life events.				
Reading (pages 31 and 36)	• I can read and understand an advertisement for a tourist attraction and a biography of a famous person.				
Grammar (pages 32 and 35)	• I can use the Past simple of regular and irregular verbs to talk about the past.				
Pronunciation (page 32)	• I can pronounce verb endings in the Past simple correctly.				
Speaking (pages 34 and 35)	• I can ask for and give reasons.				
Listening (page 36)	• I can understand a history quiz.				
Writing (page 37)	• I can give information in the correct order in a biography. • I can write a biography.				

2 What new words and expressions can I remember?

words

....

expressions

....

3 How can I practice other new words and expressions?

record them on my MP3 player ☐   write them in a notebook ☐
practice them with a friend ☐   translate them into my language ☐

4 What English have I learned outside class?

	words	expressions
on the radio		
in songs		
in movies		
on the Internet		
on TV		
with friends		

My Assessment Profile Unit

1 **What can I do? Mark (✓) the options in the table.**

⏪ = I need to study this again.　⏸ = I'm not sure about this.　▶ = I'm happy with this.　⏩ = I do this very well.

		⏪	⏸	▶	⏩
Vocabulary (pages 44 and 47)	• I can use twelve words and expressions to talk about breaking rules. • I can use eleven prepositions of movement.				
Reading (pages 45 and 50)	• I can read and understand a letter to a problem page in a magazine and a newspaper article about a crime.				
Grammar (pages 46 and 49)	• I can use the Past continuous to describe actions that were in progress at a particular time in the past. • I can use the Past simple and Past continuous with *when* and *while* to talk about an action that happened while another, longer action was taking place.				
Pronunciation (page 46)	• I can use the strong and weak forms of *was* and *were* correctly.				
Speaking (pages 48 and 49)	• I can show interest.				
Listening (page 50)	• I can understand an interview with the police.				
Writing (page 51)	• I can use sequencing words to show the order of events. • I can write a short story.				

2 **What new words and expressions can I remember?**

words

....

expressions

....

3 **How can I practice other new words and expressions?**

record them on my MP3 player	☐	write them in a notebook	☐
practice them with a friend	☐	translate them into my language	☐

4 **What English have I learned outside class?**

	words	expressions
on the radio		
in songs		
in movies		
on the Internet		
on TV		
with friends		

Notes

Notes

Notes

Notes

Pearson Education Limited
Edinburgh Gate
Harlow
Essex CM20 2JE
England
and Associated Companies throughout the world.

www.pearsonelt.com/moveit

© Pearson Education Limited 2015

The right of Jayne Wildman, Carolyn Barraclough and Suzanne Gaynor
to be identified as the authors of this work has been asserted by them in
accordance with the Copyright, Designs and Patents Act, 1988.

First published 2015
Ninth impression 2020
Set in 10.5/12.5pt LTC Helvetica Neue Light
ISBN: 978-1-2921-0133-0
Printed and bound by L.E.G.O. S.p.A. (Italy)

Photo Acknowledgements

The publisher would like to thank the following for their kind permission
to reproduce their photographs:

(Key: b-bottom; c-centre; l-left; r-right; t-top)

Students' Book:
Alamy Images: BEEPstock / Robin Beckham 59 (c), Juniors Bildarchiv
10/10, Bushpilot 10/8, Directphoto.org 59 (f), Ian Fraser 11 (b),
INTERFOTO 39 (c), Leonid Plotkin 29br, Radius Images 53tl, ZUMA Press,
Inc. 16br; **Bridgeman Art Library Ltd:** The Great Fire of London,
1666 (print) (see also 53641), Verschuier, Lieve (1630-86) (after) /
Private Collection / The Bridgeman Art Library 31; **Corbis:** 64bl, Wang
Dingchang / Xinhua Press 11 (c), William Manning 10/2, Ocean 7c;
Fotolia.com: Diego Cervo 10/4, Kalim 63l, kuosumo 63c, .shock 18,
Julien Tromeur 20/4; **Getty Images:** AFP / Jeff Haynes 10/5, Blend
Images / Andersen Ross 59 (d), Bongarts / Alex Grimm 16bc, Clive
Brunskill 16bl, Hulton Archive 37, The Image Bank / Antonio M. Rosario
20/8, MJ Kim 21 (d), Minden Pictures / Konrad Wothe 20/1, National
Geographic / Felipe Davalos 39 (b), Photographer's Choice / Still Images
10/1, Photonica / Gone Wild 59 (e), Oli Scarff 36, Cameron Spencer 17,
Matthew Stockman 16tl, Stone / Erik Dreyer 21 (c), Stone / Steve McAlister
20/5, Stone+ / Daly and Newton 20/2; **iStockphoto:** 1001nights 50,
Brainsil 7tr, Crazytang 23, cyfrogclone 19, Eva-Katalin 41, Juanmonino
20/7, KJA 64tr, nyul 21tl, oblanchko 29tr, 53tr, Arkadiy Yarmolenko
10/12; **Pearson Education Ltd:** 7tc; **Pearson Education Ltd:** Jon
Barlow 24, 59t, Gareth Boden 7b, 8tl, 8tc, 8br, 9, 14, 22, 34, 48b, 58,
60, 61; **Photolibrary.com:** Action Plus 10/9, Age Fotostock / Douglas
Williams 59 (b), Age Fotostock / George Shelley 45, Age Fotostock
/ Liane Cary 63r, AGE fotostock / Rick Gomez 7cr, fStop 10/3, Glow
Images, Inc 10/6, Image100 7cl, Imagebroker.net / Karl F Schofmann 21
(a), Imagebroker.net / Markus Keller 33, Loop Images / Eric Nathan 51,
Novastock 59 (a); **Press Association Images:** AP / Matt Rourke 53br;
Rex Features: P. Anastasselis 29tl, Miquel Benitez 26, KPA / Zuma 11 (a),
Sipa Press 16tr; **Shutterstock.com:** Yuri Arcurs 21 (b), Alexey Boldin 48tl,
Bogdan Ionescu 48tr, Monkey Business Images 7tl, Regien Paassen 64br,
Dmitriy Shironosov 10/7, versh 10/11; **The Kobal Collection:** BBC Films
20/3, Morgan Creek / Jon Farmer 20/6, United Artists / Saeed Adyani 27

Workbook:
Alamy Images: Bushpilot 72bl, PicturesofLondon 70/1, Radius Images
102, Adrian Sherratt 86; **Corbis:** Aflo / Koji Aoki 73, Comet / Jutta Klee
96, 122, Corbis Yellow 79, 80, 121, Ocean 74, Spirit / Lawrence Manning
72tl, Tetra Images 71br; **Fotolia.com:** 71/7, 71/9, 72tc, 72cr, 87, 116bc,
120, 123, 127-131; **Getty Images:** AFP / Jeff Haynes 72br, ColorBlind
Images / Iconica 70/4, Digital Vision 117t, Hill Street Studios / Blend
Images 99, i love images / Cultura 117bl, Photodisc / Andersen Ross 117br,
Photodisc / Jena Cumbo 70/3, Still Images 72c; **Pearson Education
Ltd:** 70/2, 70/5, 70/6, 71/1, 71/2, 71/3, 71/4, 71/5, 71/6, 71/8, 83, 90,
103, 116cl; **Photolibrary.com:** Action Plus 72tr, fStop 72cl; **Sébastien
Foucan:** Jon Lucas 78; **Shutterstock.com:** Stephen Coburn 93, Corepics
VOF 116cr, dotshock 116tr, Happy Together 116tl, imtmphoto 106, versh
72bc; **SuperStock:** Gallo Images 70/8, i love images 97, Universal Images
Group 94, View Pictures Ltd 70/7

Cover images: *Front:* **Shutterstock.com:** Sebastian Duda

All other images © Pearson Education

Every effort has been made to trace the copyright holders and we
apologise in advance for any unintentional omissions. We would be
pleased to insert the appropriate acknowledgement in any subsequent
edition of this publication.

Special thanks to the following for their help during location
photography:
Birchwood High School, Bishop's Stortford; The Evans family; Freeport
Outlet Shopping Village; Ganesha, London; Number Ten Bowling; J K
Palmers, St Albans; St Albans School; Tower of London and Historic Royal
Palaces.

Illustrated by

Students' Book:
Alfonso Abad; Sonia Alins; Maxwell Dorsey; Paula Franco;
Kate Rochester.

Workbook:
Alfonso Abad; Sonia Alins; Moreno Chiacchiera; Paula Franco;
Kate Rochester.